dda exchange

dda exchange was founded as the "house organ" and employee newsletter for the CIA's internal business administration directorate. Commonly referred to as DDA, the Deputy Directorate for Administration was one of four main directorates (along with Intelligence, Operations, and Science & Technology) comprising the Agency's organizational structure in the mid-1970s.

This was a relatively unglamorous era for the intelligence community: the Church Committee investigations following Watergate forced the Agency, for the first time in its history, to publicly disclose its chthonic undertakings, including MKULTRA and Operation CHAOS, and these excesses prompted Congress to rein in the long leash they'd given the boys (and girls) at Langley for decades. Black budgets suddenly saw the light of day. Incriminating paperwork was dredged up. Names were named.

dda exchange is, in essence, the "new" and "reformed" CIA of 1976 announcing itself to its employees, replete with an image makeover and rebrand courtesy of the Photography & Printing Division. DDA Exchange's readership constituted the institutional backbone of the Agency, employees with a wide range of command over the CIA's human resources, budgeting, security (including personnel security clearances and facility security), communication infrastructure, training, and medical services. They managed the day-to-day operations, from payroll and procurement to the management of cover arrangements for officers serving overseas.

The DDA was the CIA's nerve center, the inter-departmental switchboard and memorandum clearing house powering the Agency. So the material included in each issue of this "quarterly publication for the exchange among DDA personnel of ideas, concepts, information, and techniques that are of common interest" covers a fascinating swath of the mundane and clandestine. Featured articles include executive-level commentary such as "ITS TIME TO FIGHT BACK - Public Affairs at the CIA," on-the-ground profiles of the Agency's couriers and truck drivers, personnel primers covering home security procedures and document destruction , and the "Major Challenges" of 1979, in which the Communication department laments that "overseas perks are disappearing" amid "inflation and the shrinking dollar along with crime and terrorism abroad."

The duties and responsibilities of the DDA also covered management of the Agency's computing resources, offering an unparalleled view into the digital mire of a rapidly modernizing intelligence apparatus. Even as early as 1976 the CIA boasted of their "Generalized Information Management System" (GIMS) which allowed personnel to "search for information on foreign military targets, foreign individuals, and telemetry data" using an English-like query language. But by the 1980s the exponential pace and ferocity of the free market surprised even the highest brass at Langley. As the Chief of Processing Analysis Technology writes, "We are in the midst of an information revolution, which, like the industrial revolution before it, will change the way we do our jobs, the jobs we do, and the organizational context in which we do them. Wistfully, this is one revolution where our Agency will not be in the van."

But perhaps the most striking aspect of this publication is its design and layout. At first glance it could be mistaken for an Art & Project Bulletin or some glossy gallery text from a Berlin kunsthalle. With a largesse drawn from the National Endowment for the Arts, the Photography & Printing Division went all out with their high-modern brutalist vision for **dda exchange**: stark black and white across acres of negative space with an Avant Garde logotype and tightly-justified body text, everything spaced out on a sparse grid intermittently stamped with grainy black and white photography and vector line graphics. It's a remarkable package and, to this editor's mind, only reinforces the aesthetic acumen that allowed the Agency to infiltrate every major American arts movement of the 20th century.

One final note: you may consider this book as an omnibus digest of **dda exchange**, printed in facsimile form accounting for the specifications outlined in the original design document. I've included excerpts from every available issue I could find, dating from the first issue in April 1976 to the last publicly disclosed issue, February 1981. All this material and more is available via the CIA's Reading Room.

See you on the other side.

SECRET

april 1976

dda exchange

SECRET

comment

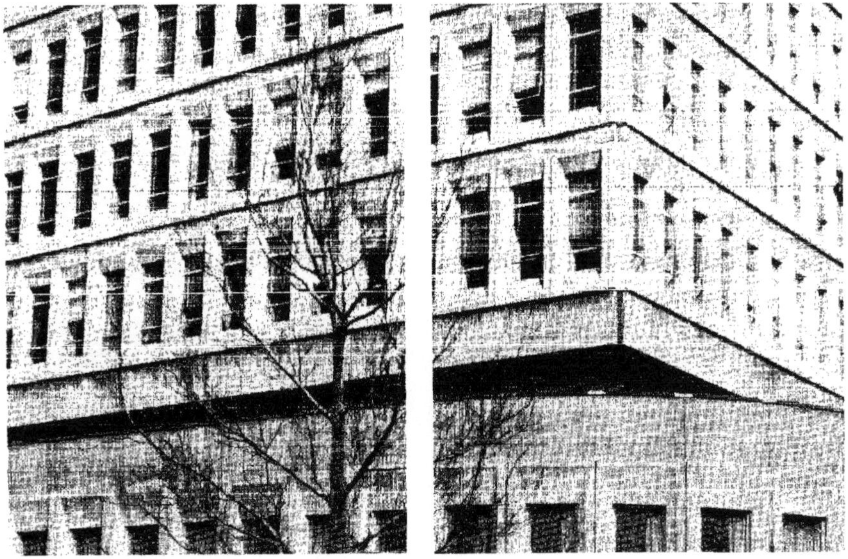

A brief comment might be in order to launch this periodical on what is hoped will be a long and productive life. I think it is important to know that a great deal of thought went into naming the publication. Webster's *Unabridged Dictionary* provides a variety of definitions for the word, "exchange," but the one most appropriate for this issue is "reciprocal giving and receiving." This describes pretty much the elusive goal of communications.

If there is one concept that pervades our thinking, it is how to communicate better—how to get information spread throughout the Directorate—both up and down, and sideways. This process it seems to me must be reciprocal—must involve give and take—in a word, "exchange."

Over the years many schemes or systems have been used to facilitate communications. Some have been good, some not so good. I'm not sure any have withstood the test of time. We hope EXCHANGE will, and will serve a most useful purpose in helping to pass the word. It is not the only vehicle, but hopefully it will be one of the most useful and most sought after.

It seems clear to me that the essence of the definition "exchange" is vital to the success of this publication—reciprocal giving and receiving. No magazine or journal can be successful without the enthusiastic (and knowledgeable) effort of its contributors. The articles which you provide, must be well written, well thought out, of interest to a rather broad audience and must bear a stamp of enthusiasm. Without it, the idea is doomed to failure. With it, we hope to have EXCHANGE become a sought after, informative document. The strength of your contributions will directly and in equal proportion affect the value which you will receive from the publication.

We have high hopes for EXCHANGE and we expect our DDA readership to "give and to receive reciprocally."

John F. Blake
Deputy Director of Administration

vol. 1, no. 1

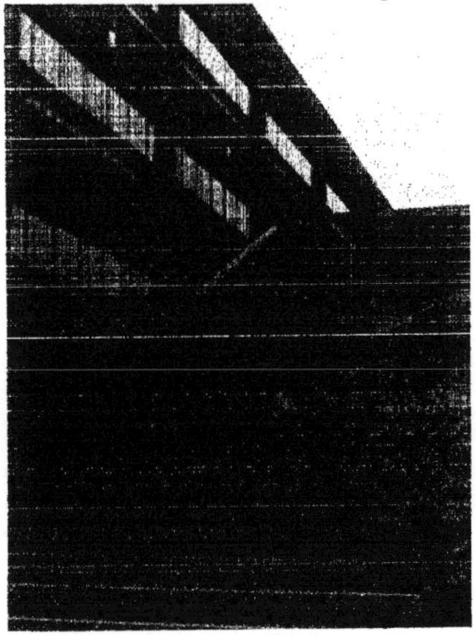

Today in the Directorate of Administration the psychologist edits his study on terrorist behavior; the recruiter interviews job applicants at the University of California; the auditor approves a claim for payment under a classified, multi-million dollar research contract; the security escort shepherds the DCI to the Hill; the courier rushes the just-off-the-press National Intelligence Daily to the White House; the instructor unveils the mystery of Swahili verbs to his students; the communicator selects an alternate route because the Atlantic satellite has a problem; the operator instructs the computer to plot the trajectory of a Russian test missile; and the coordinator denies a citizen all files on the Bay of Pigs. The daily operations within our Directorate are diverse and, superficially, bear little resemblance to one another. However, we share a common responsibility for administration of Agency-wide programs and providing effective and economical management of resources. In these areas we strive toward similar goals and wrestle with like problems.

Communicating is at best a difficult process. It is a special challenge to the DDA with our heterogeneous organizations, physical dispersion, and disparate interests. The DDA Planning Team, an informal organization of representatives from each of the offices, that is committed to improving communications, is sponsoring EXCHANGE—"A publication designed to furnish a medium for the exchange of ideas, concepts, information, and techniques that are of common interest to the personnel who are engaged in resource management in the Directorate of Administration."

DDA-PS

forum

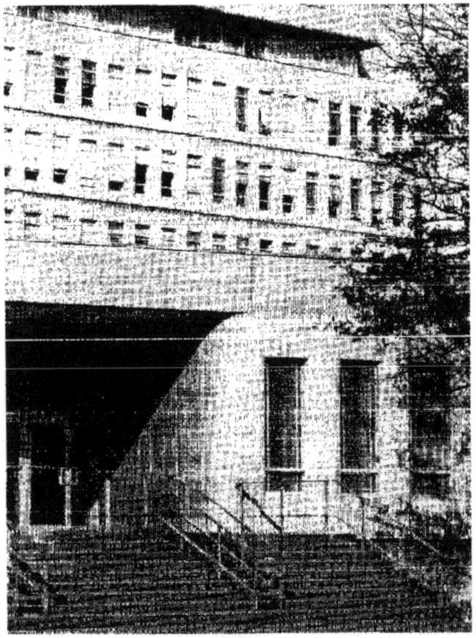

The forum in ancient Rome was the place to discuss matters of public interest. The forum here is a place to discuss matters of common interest to DDA resource managers.

security

PERSONNEL PROTECTION PROGRAM

The people who killed Richard Welch on 23 December 1975 in front of his home in Athens belong to a not-too-exclusive and ever growing club. They go by the name of "terrorists." Terror is their game. Terror is their product. And they have been moving their product at an awesome rate.

Since January 1968, 65 members of the American official community in 16 foreign countries have been either attacked, kidnapped, held for ransom and/or killed. Those attacked or killed include nine officers of ambassadorial rank. Concern for the safety of American officials abroad reached a peak when Ambassador Noel and DCM Moore were assassinated in March 1973 in Khartoum, Sudan. The kidnappings and killings have continued. The recent murder of an Iranian by dissident elements in Tehran was later discovered to be an error: the intended victim was an Agency officer. That murder and the assassination of Richard Welch emphasize that Agency personnel are now being specifically targetted for assassination. These murders, coupled with the continued public identification of CIA personnel, are considered sufficient to warrant a concerted effort on the part of the Agency, and OS in particular, to run a program to provide Agency personnel with training and guidance to counter the threat to themselves and their dependents.

For many years, OS has, of course, routinely addressed the problem of protecting Agency installations overseas. In recent years, greater emphasis has been directed toward protecting Agency personnel against terrorist attacks. A training program is now offered to all personnel departing for overseas which deals with safety in the residence. Where the terrorist threat has been extreme special teams have been sent to installations to provide advice and guidance on personnel protection. Such [redacted]

The current terrorist threat appears to pervade all phases of the overseas environment. This thrust and the increased tempo have caused OS to undertake a program to address the problem on a priority basis in all of its facets. The result is that OS is now dispatching two-man teams on a world-wide basis to visit Agency residences, to counsel personnel, to study personnel habit patterns which might play into the hands of terrorists. Eight such teams were in the field as of 1 April. The program has been welcomed with considerable enthusiasm by those stations visited thus far.

OS

personnel

THE PROJECTION OF AGE DISTRIBUTION MODEL

The Office of Personnel periodically analyzes on-duty professional personnel to determine the age distribution of the professional population. Frequently, the analysis has involved some tedious hand counts and computations. During the past year, however, a computer-based model programed in the Dynamo language has been used to facilitate the analysis.

The System Dynamic methodology was used to design the model. It is based on the assumption that there is a relationship between the number of persons in an age group and the number of persons who flow in and out of that age group as a result of aging, accessions and separations.

The model was used first to project the effect of several different management policies on the age distribution of the on-duty professional personnel. For example, OP wanted to find out what the impact would be if a particular directorate hired various numbers of professionals. The managers in that directorate were considering three alternatives they could follow between 1 July 75 and 30 June 80:

hire 50 in FY 76 and 70 each year thereafter;

training

CENTER FOR THE STUDY OF INTELLIGENCE

The past year has witnessed the experimental development within the DDA of a radically new Agency concept, authorized by the Management Committee, and aimed at the advancement of Agency professionalism. Within OTR, the Center for the Study of Intelligence has been established as a kind of Agency "think tank" designed to research and discuss issues and problems involving the basic processes and functions of intelligence including collection, production and support. The basic objective of the research and discussion is to contribute to the expanding professional literature of intelligence. The Center hopefully will contribute to the description and clarification of existing intelligence processes, and will serve as one focal point for the articulation of suggested change.

The first of the Center products, a study of *CIA Intelligence Support for Foreign and National Security Policy Making* was distributed within the Agency in January and has stimulated considerable discussion and debate on this important intelligence process. The study was produced over a nine-month period by a three-man team of "research fellows" working on full-time detail from their parent offices. Under the Center concept, all research studies will be produced by such fellows—volunteer intelligence officers from across the Agency assigned full time to the Center for the duration of a specific study. The permanent staff at the Center consists of a research director to give continuity and detailed guidance to the program and a small support element. With the assistance of the DDA, a Board of Advisors, consisting of ten senior Agency officials was organized to set overall policy for the Center and to assist in its development. The Board is chaired by the ADDA.

At present, work is well along at the Center on team studies of the CIA field station of the future and on an examination of the impact of compartmentation in the Agency. Officers from the DDO, DDA and DDI are participating. Planning is under way for a study of the CIA estimative intelligence process. It is envisioned that about ten fellows will be working at the Center at any one time. Several additional fellows will be needed for new projects during 1976. Nominations for projects and personnel for the Center are being solicited from interested individual officers and from Agency components.

A series of group discussions, seminars, and conferences among Agency officers on professional intelligence issues is also being sponsored by the Center. So far, these have mainly concentrated on issues associated with intelligence analysis, including its multidisciplinary aspects. Day-long conferences on such processes as intelligence requirements are currently being planned.

At the end of its first year, the concept of the intelligence study center certainly seems promising enough to initiate a second round of research and discussion projects in 1976. Its success will hinge ultimately on its value to the Agency at large as judged by the response to its product and activities. This response in turn will depend upon the relevance and utility to the Agency of Center activities and on the caliber and interest of the fellows attracted to the Center.

[redacted] OTR

EDITORIAL COMMENT

The DDA Representative is Mr. [redacted]. [redacted]

computer support

COMPUTER TERMINALS

There is a heavy demand from computer service users for computer terminals. This article provides some insight into this demand and its impact. A few measures are suggested that would conserve ADP resources and provide some improvement in services to terminal users.

Early Uses of Computer Terminals

Computer terminals were first used on OJCS computer systems in 1967. By November 1968, some indication of the potential growth in the demand for terminals could be seen. Some of the first uses of terminals were for system and program development in OJCS, name searches in OS, and scientific intelligence problems in OEL and OWI. Installation of terminals required arranging for physical security in the user's office and running data communication lines from the computer to the terminal. In OJCS, the pressures were on development of software and installation of additional computer equipment to support new applications and greater numbers of terminals.

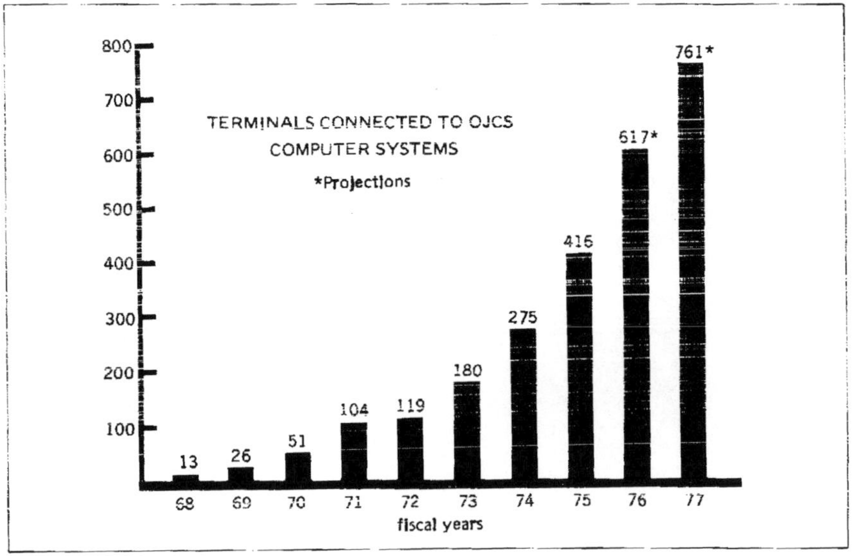
TERMINALS CONNECTED TO OJCS
COMPUTER SYSTEMS
*Projections
800
700
600
500
400
300
200
100
13
26
51
104
119
180
275
416
617*
761*
68
69
70
71
72
73
74
75
76
77
fiscal years

IN CONCLUSION

You have just finished leafing through this first issue of EXCHANGE. What do you think of it?

Is there an article with which you disagree or which you think is incomplete? Set us straight with your side of the story.

Do you have any suggestions for improvement in format, illustrations, length of articles, etc.? Thanks, but no centerfold.

Is there a subject which you would like to read about? Pass on your suggestions.

Do you have a manuscript or graphics on a subject of interest to EXCHANGE readers? Submit it.

How about any specific or general compliments? Air mail these.

The Senior Editor for your Office is listed on page 1. He will thank you for your contributions—written or verbal—and your support. Only through feedback can we hone EXCHANGE to meet your interests. Please don't be shy about speaking up.

H. A. V.

secret

Directorate of Administration

secret

secret

AMERICAN REVOLUTION BICENTENNIAL 1776-1976

july 1976

dda exchange

secret

"All our actions should be regulated by one uniform Plan—& that Plan should have one object only in view, to wit, the good of the Service. Where this is the case, although there may be a diversity of opinion, there can be no real obstruction.—I hope all these little rubs will be done away by your prudent management."

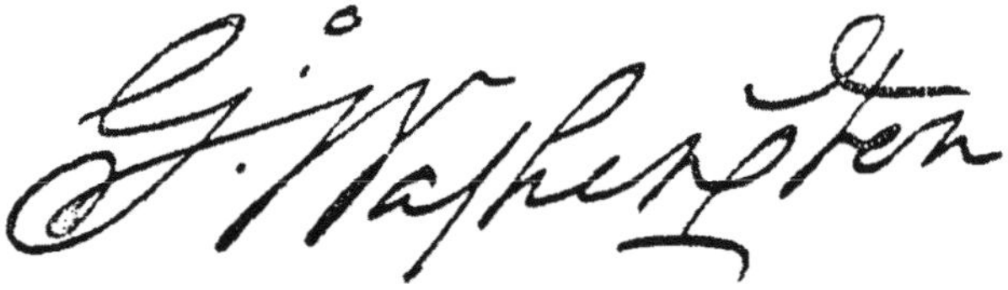

George Washington in a letter to Brig. Gen. Varnum, 4 November 1777

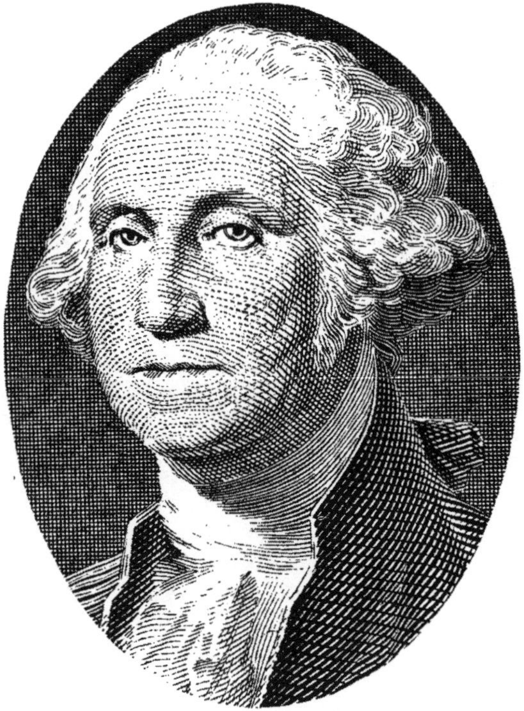

25X1

staff

A publication designed to furnish a medium for the exchange of ideas, concepts, information, and techniques that are of common interest to the personnel who are engaged in resource management in the Directorate of Administration.

index

NATIONAL SECURITY INFORMATION

Unauthorized Disclosure Subject to Criminal Sanctions

comment

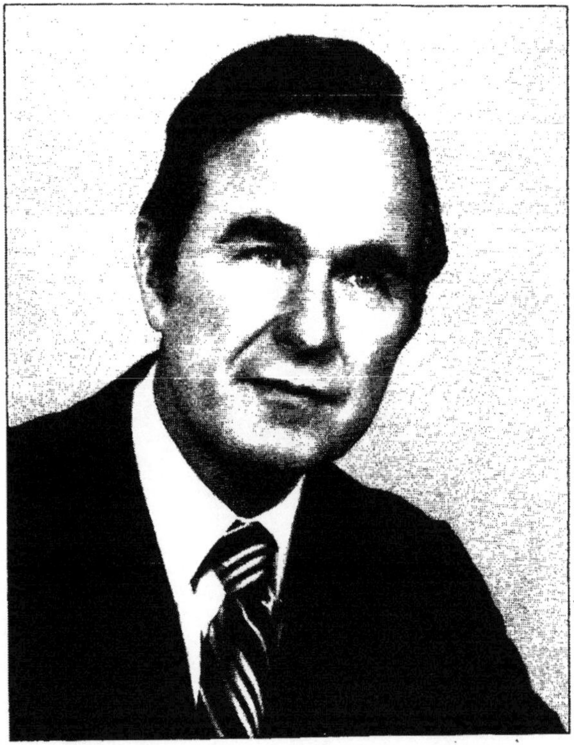

George Bush
Director

It is a real pleasure for me to write a few words for *Exchange*. I am deeply committed to the premise that we in the Agency must have better communications with one another. I believe that innovative approaches such as this magazine are just the sort of thing that we need to stimulate discussion and provide a sounding board for new ideas.

In the months since I became Director, I have been continually impressed with the quality of the people in this Agency. There is a great willingness to think about new ways to do things; to try new approaches. Flexibility and imagination have always been the hallmarks of the Agency, and I hope all of you will join me in ensuring that we continue to go forward with the same spirit of dedication.

I have had some opportunity to travel around the country as Director, and I have everywhere found a great reservoir of support for the Agency. The American people do understand the need for intelligence, and they realize how difficult and demanding our task is. I am very proud to be part of the Agency and very happy to be working with you. [redacted]

vol. 1, no. 2

THE DDA . . . 200 YEARS AGO

Since this issue coincides with the Bicentennial celebration, it might be fun to look at the Revolutionary War period and see how the DDA might have done. Credit for the following must be given [redacted] Curator of the Historical Intelligence Collection.

Personnel

George Washington insisted that personnel engaged for the Intelligence Service be men of "inginuity and integrity." It is clear that he sought out specialists for assignments when such skills were needed. An example was James Bowdoin, a scientist of some renown who was sent to Halifax, Nova Scotia, for information on fortifications. Bowdoin returned with detailed plans of the harbor, including water depths. General Washington insisted that American intelligence personnel be those "suitable persons . . . to whom a confidence may be reposed."

Security

The Continental Congress exercised strict security in regard to intelligence, to the point of maintaining a "Secret Journal" of proceedings which could not be made public, of hearing certain reports under injunction of secrecy, of deleting names of intelligence sources from reports presented for their attention, and of adopting a resolution signed personally by members present declaring that any member of that body guilty of unauthorized disclosure of secrets would be expelled and declared an enemy.

On the military front, General Washington resorted to severe penalties including the lash for security violations. Washington's interest in security, in secrecy, is reflected in the following quote. "The necessity of procuring good intelligence is apparent, and need not be further urged—all that remains for me to add is that you keep the whole matter as secret as possible. For upon Secrecy, Success depends in most enterprises of the kind, and for want of it, they are generally defeated . . ."

Communications

The use of codes and ciphers was not a new experience for American intelligence during the Revolutionary War. Codes and code books were devised. Robert Morris devised a cipher for communication with George Washington. Unfamiliarity with dealing with codes and ciphers is best expressed by the Marquis de la Fayette in a postscript to a message: ". . . I beg you to excuse the awkwardness and the bad construction of my ciphers; I am very new at this business, and I fear I have made them as unintelligible to you as they would be to Mylord Howe . . ."

Training

It has been said that after the ill-fated mission of Captain Nathan Hale into British-occupied New York, George Washington vowed that never again would an agent be dispatched without proper training, mission instruction, and preparation. Giving instructions for an intelligence operation, Washington advised General Mifflin to get the proper persons to undertake the task, and to set about immediately giving the persons proper lessons. Washington's wartime correspondence reflects his strong advocacy of intelligence tradecraft. A number of his letters give effective guidance on double agent operations, intercepting of British intelligence pouches, flaps and seals, secret writing, etc.

Finance

Although the Board of Treasury of the Continental Congress suffered from what has been kindly referred to as "imperfect management," George Washington imposed strict accountability on funds used for intelligence. At the conclusion of the conflict, Washington submitted his accounting, including, in a sense, a covert payroll in that Washington declined to insert the names of agents to whom payments had been made. The intelligence-related "early warning" ride of Paul Revere was followed by a detailed travel voucher claiming expenses, including per diem. The voucher was not approved for some months, and then only after his per diem was reduced from five to four shillings a day.

Computer Support

Many classical techniques of data arrangement and tabulation were in existence during the American Revolution. General Washington instructed one of his intelligence officers to "make out a table or something in the way of columns under which you might range their (the enemy's) magazines of forage, grain and the like, the different corps and regiments, the Works, where thrown up, their connexion, kind and extent, the officers commanding with the number of guns, etc." This instruction was followed by a sample form devised by Washington to be used in the tabulation of intelligence data.

Medical Services

Congress established the post of Director General of Hospitals. The Directors, during the war, struggled with lack of medical personnel, inadequate supplies, and small appropriations by the Continental Congress.

In the foreign intelligence area, the first secret intelligence agent employed in Britain by the Committee of Secret Correspondence was Arthur Lee, M.D., and the "sympathetic stain" (secret ink) used by Washington in agent communication was the creation of James Jay, M.D.

Logistics

Covert procurement during the Revolution was handled by the "Secret Committee" of the Continental Congress. The Committee had wide powers and large sums of money and was charged not only with procurement of military supplies, but also their distribution to the military forces, the colonies, and the privateers. It kept its transactions secret and even destroyed many of its records to assure that the confidentiality of its work was maintained. It employed agents in Europe to arrange the secret supply of war material, secured assistance from the French through a cover company, and gained necessary supplies and assistance from the Spanish in New Orleans and elsewhere.

The above, of course, are vignettes of administration of intelligence during the Revolutionary War. They are sufficient to reflect certain consistencies despite the passing of 200 years. [redacted]

A[redacted] EO-DD/A

Below—Paul Revere's travel order
Right—His travel voucher

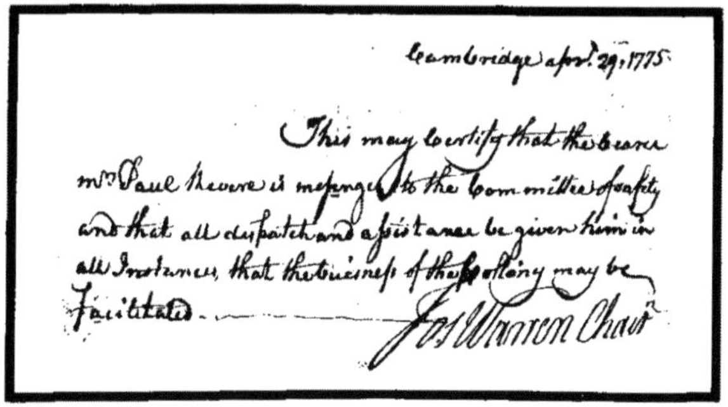

Cambridge apr. 29, 1775

This may certify that the bearer Mr Paul Revere is messenger to the Committee of safety and that all dispatch and assistance be given him in all Instances, that the business of the Colony may be Facilitated. Jos Warren Chair

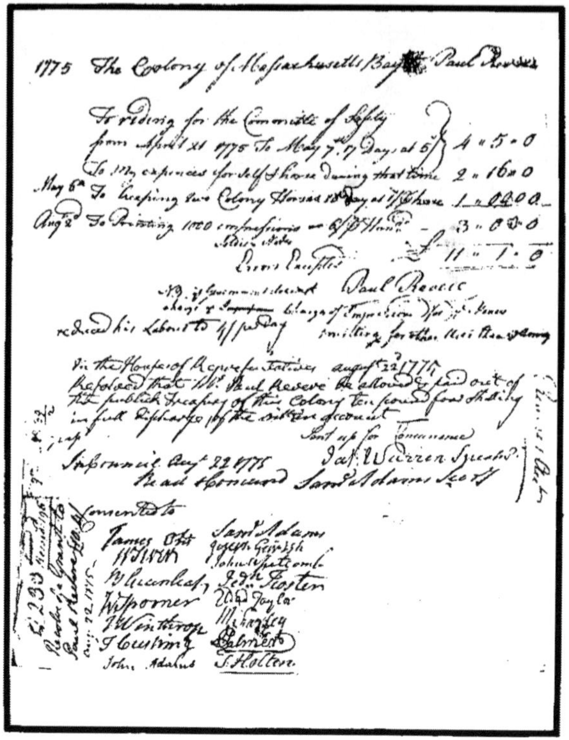

1775 The Colony of Massachusetts Bay to Paul Revere

To riding for the Committee of Safety from April 21 1775 to May 7th 17 Days at 5/ — 4 „ 5 „ 0
To My expences for self & horse during that time — 2 „ 16 „ 0
May 6th To keeping two Colony Horses 18 Days at 1/ each horse — 1 „ 00 „ 0
Aug 2d To Printing 1000 impressions — 3 „ 0 „ 0
£ 11 „ 1 „ 0

Errors Excepted
Paul Revere

In the House of Representatives August 22d 1775
Resolved that Mr. Paul Revere be allowed & paid out of the publick Treasury of this Colony ten pounds four shillings in full discharge of the within account
Sent up for Concurrence
Jas. Warren Speaker

In Council Aug. 22 1775
Read & Concurred Saml Adams Secy

Consented to
James Otis — Saml Adams
W Sever — Joseph Gerrish
B Greenleaf — John Whitcomb
W Spooner — Jedh Foster
J Winthrop — Eldad Taylor
T Cushing — M Farley
John Adams — S Holten

forum

"Administration is . . ."

training

THE MEDIA CENTER

Have you ever seen a board-walk? Have you ever seen a butter-fly? Have you ever seen a Media Center? Why not? It's there in GJ-68 Headquarters. The Media Center opened in January 1975 and is available for your benefit 24 hours a day.

Your benefit is the improvement of your mind by means of a self-study program. By using the audio or video equipment available you can become acquainted with subjects such as Management by Objectives, Speed Reading, Communicating Successfully, Effective Writing and others that can lead you into the world of knowledge in a most delightful way.

Or do you have that unquenchable desire to delve into the exotic languages of the world? Don't waste your lunch hour with plain food but partake of the food for the mind and listen to that language on the audio cassettes.

25X1A

Maybe your shorthand has fallen off and the need to keep your hard earned skill up to par is your desire. The Media Center can help you with timed practice tapes.

Perhaps that routine conference can be livened up with the aid of a videocassette and the Media Center's mobile unit. As the title suggests the unit is self-contained and completely mobile within the Headquarters Building. A call to the Center ([redacted] a few days in advance to reserve the unit is all it takes to get everyone's undivided attention at that all important meeting.

All you ever wanted to know about the computer is available on videocassettes. Under the auspices of OJCS, the Media Center is well supplied to take you where you need to be in this field. There is also a new program starting soon on a trial basis—the *Focus* programs put out with the combined efforts of the Brookings Institution and The Carnegie Endowment for International Peace.

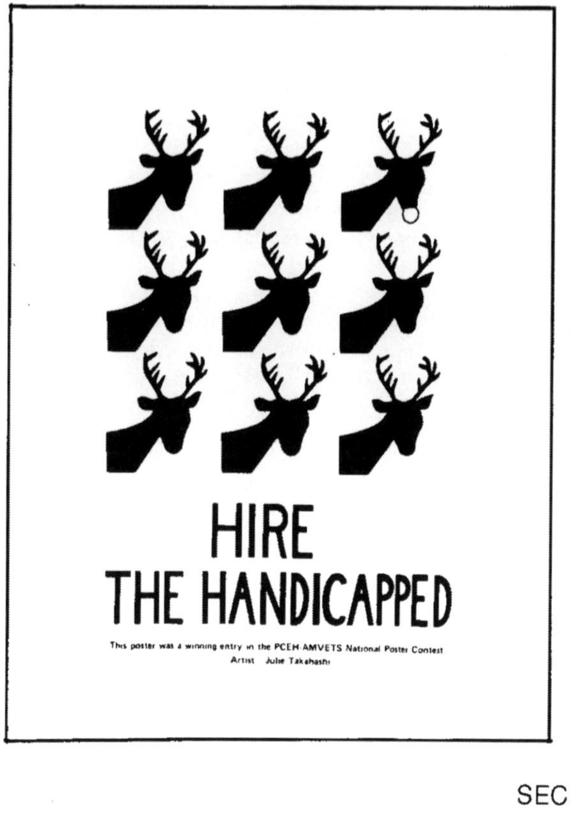

In OJCS, OP, and OS employees are learning sign language, either on their own, from their deaf co-workers, in Agency-sponsored outside courses, or more recently, in a formal in-house course. An OS employee provides sign language interpreter services for applicant interviews, escorting and assisting them through various appointments, and assisting them through the entrance on duty processing. OJCS has purchased a telephone attachment (TTY) which helps their deaf employees to communicate with the office from their homes. The OTR Media Center has initiated action to obtain instructional sign language material for the Center. OL and OC have submitted requirements to OP to fill specific jobs with individuals who have handicaps. So we are making progress—and the more experience we have in working with and getting to know persons who have handicaps, the more likely it is that the attitudinal barriers will also come down. With the example set by these several DDA Offices and employees, and with the advice and assistance of the newly-formed Handicapped Program

computer support

GENERALIZED INFORMATION MANAGEMENT SYSTEM

Do you have thousands of pieces of information that you need rapid access to? Do you often spend hours searching this information because of a variety of questions you receive? Are you frustrated because your set of information relates closely with data owned by others, and you are unable to bring the two together?

These are the types of questions that OJCS asks its customers when deciding if the GIMS software package can help solve their problem. GIMS (Generalized Information Management System) was written by [redacted] and OJCS has been using it since 25X1
1972.

The characteristics that make GIMS unique are:

User has access to his data via terminals.

Many users can be accessing the same files simultaneously.

An English-like language is available for queries and update.

One update or query transaction can cause many records in different files to be updated or searched.

There are now 19 computer systems supported by GIMS. The number of users connected to GIMS averages about 45 and during periods of high activity this number will reach 60. These applications fall into the categories of Business, Tracking and Analytical Systems.

Business Systems

Nine of the 19 systems support the administrative needs of the Agency. These systems update and provide information on budget data, inventory control, personnel data, contract data, badges, special clearances, and control of medical records. All but one of these systems directly support a DDA component.

Each of these systems has its own updating and reporting cycle, and yet they are dependent on each other for proper support. For example, a list of valid projects is maintained in the budget system. On a periodic basis, this file is passed to the inventory and personnel GIMS. The GIMS file also feeds data to non-GIMS projects.

Tracking Systems

GIMS projects are tracking work requests in OJCS and IAS/DDI and case processing in OS. These applications allow the user to update his files as work is received, processed, and completed. The user can check the status of any job or summarize the flow of work in a variety of formats.

Analytical Files

DDI components search GIMS files for information on foreign military targets, foreign individuals and telemetry data of missiles. The analysts scan the files and ask questions on a wide variety of fields. For example, user analysts search foreign individual files and ask on-line questions on a specific name, organization, and location. The user is able to initially search the files within broad areas. He then is able to continually refine the search criteria until the correct population of records is selected.

The two concerns that any on-line user has are:

Availability—how often will I be able to access data?

Response Time—will there be wide fluctuations in the time that answers are returned to the terminal?

The issue of availability centers around the redundancy of hardware. Many "black boxes" serially connected together must operate correctly for the user to receive his data. Each component has a high reliability level, but the total reliability of the series of components is significantly lower. Redundant components are expensive and are difficult to justify when budgets are tight.

The changes in response time are primarily due to the number of users on the system. On-line systems have a maximum threshold of users. When the number is exceeded, response time increases. This condition is most obvious during budget exercises when a high volume of activity occurs in a short time span. A major hardware upgrade for GIMS users will occur this summer that should allow more users on the system with a more predictable response time.

In conclusion, the GIMS software has been used on a variety of user problems and OJCS projections show a continuous rise in the use of the software. It has proven to be a valuable tool by allowing users better access to their data. [redacted]

[redacted] OJCS

medical services

TERRORISM AND THE BICENTENNIAL YEAR

Opportunities for terrorist assaults on national and international targets abound during this Bicentennial year. Attractive targets include the Bicentennial celebrations, the Canadian Olympics in Montreal, and the presidential nominating conventions.

Across the country crowds are assembling for Bicentennial celebrations and virtually every head of state has been invited to participate in Bicentennial festivities both here and abroad. Americans living overseas are planning parties at embassies and consulates to celebrate America's 200th birthday.

No matter how well protected, a visiting head of state or a high-ranking U. S. official is still a prime target for a terrorist assassination or kidnapping. The kidnappings of the OPEC oil ministers in December are examples of the successful kidnapping of high level officials.

Often, however, potential victims are not as important as the message. A glorified public image, provided by the media, can encourage already existing subversive elements in a society. By taking advantage of the press coverage that accompanies historic events, revolutionaries committing violent acts prey on the fears of a nation. These acts are often designed to demonstrate a government's impotence and thereby cause people to lose confidence in their government.

Members of terrorist organizations around the world are, in many instances, well educated and from predominantly middle class families. The capabilities and motivations of these individuals vary. Doctors and lawyers and other professionals, such as those belonging to the "radical chic," often support terrorist-oriented organizations. In the United States the number of individuals dedicated to terrorism is small, but there are symphathizers who will hide them and provide logistical support for mounting attacks.

[redacted]

Students of terrorism have been taught that there are numerous and easy ways to inflict considerable damage upon a nation—even to the point of bringing governments to a halt. In addition to the tried and true techniques of bombings, kidnappings, hijackings, and assassinations, there are other potential terrorist targets. For example, commercial airlines, nuclear power plants, electric power grids—especially key transformer stations—and large oil refineries, are possible targets for a revolutionary bent on achieving his goal through a terrorist act.

Obviously there is no easy way to eliminate the threat of terrorist attack. However, examining vulnerabilities and maintaining good intelligence as well as recognizing the importance of effective management of terrorist incidents, it may be possible to make terrorism more difficult and less successful.

[redacted] 25X

Editor's note: [redacted] is a member of the 25X OMS Task Force on Counterterrorism which provides behavioral science support in the management of terrorist incidents to appropriate Agency components and members of the Intelligence Community. 25X

[redacted]

Photos furnished by OTS/DDS&T

25X1A

has come to put more of our dollars and people under objectives so that the evaluation process of those objectives can be neatly tied together. Effectiveness evaluation is here. [redacted] Only)

John N. McMahon, AD/DCI/IC

Editor's note: Condensation of remarks made by former A-DD/A, John N. McMahon, at the DD/A Planning Team Symposium on 4 May 1976.

finance

GAS—THE NEW GENERAL ACCOUNTING SYSTEM

There's a new excitement in OF about a profound change that is about to happen. A new, computerized General Accounting System (GAS) has been developed and is in the testing phase with implementation scheduled for 1 October 1976.

This system has been under development since February 1974, and represents a major effort by personnel from OF and OJCS, working as a team, in producing what is reported to be one of the most advanced accounting systems in the government today.

GAS will bring to the Agency many desirable and innovative features. One of these features is a new key-to-disk data entry system which consists of video display terminals connected to a minicomputer. This data entry system will perform validation checks, data generation and other automatic functions which are not available in the keypunch data entry mode of the current system. These new capabilities will permit GAS to edit and reject erroneous data and thereby improve the accuracy and quality of financial data processed by the new system.

GAS will substantially reduce the need for recording repetitive data on vouchers. There are two major subsystems, the Obligation Data Base and the General Ledger

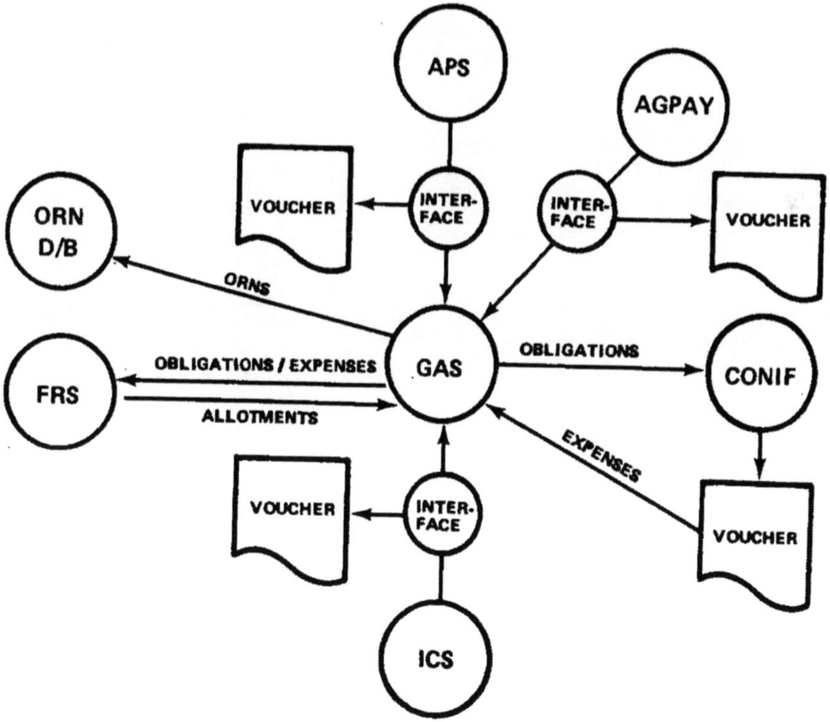
APS
AGPAY
VOUCHER
INTER-FACE
INTER-FACE
VOUCHER
ORN D/B
ORNS
GAS
OBLIGATIONS
CONIF
FRS
OBLIGATIONS / EXPENSES
ALLOTMENTS
EXPENSES
VOUCHER
INTER-FACE
VOUCHER
ICS

Data Base. A primary concept of GAS requires that most of the data pertaining to a transaction will be captured at the time of obligation and stored in the Obligation Data Base. When subsequent advances and expenses occur, the required data elements will be drawn from the Obligation Data Base, thus eliminating the need for redundant input of data on both obligations and vouchers.

An additional design concept of GAS provides for the utilization of data that is resident in other computer systems. This is accomplished through a unique device known as intersystem communication. Through this method GAS will both provide data to and be supplied with data from other Agency systems. The Automated Payroll System (APS) will provide payroll data; the Contract Information System (CONIF) will provide expense data on contracts and in turn will be provided by GAS with contract obligation data; the Inventory Control System (ICS) will provide data on encumbrances and issues; and the Financial Resources System (FRS) will provide GAS with allotment data while being provided by GAS with data relating to obligations, expenditures, encumbrances and issues to meet FRS requirements for trends and other budgetary reporting.

Transaction codes will be introduced to the Agency's accounting system for the first time. There are two types of transaction codes in GAS. One type affects the Obligation Data Base by establishing or changing data concerning obligations. The other is the transaction code which will generate entries in the General Ledger Data Base. A key feature of GAS is the concept of inputting financial data by the use of a three digit transaction code with each transaction code corresponding to a specific financial transaction. In utilizing the proper transaction code, all necessary general ledger entries are generated by the system to record a specific transaction. For example, if an advance of funds is desired, Transaction Code 010 automatically debits the appropriate advance account based on the "Type Advance" shown on the ORN Data Base and credits a cash account.

Perhaps the most significant advantages of the new system are centered in the area of timeliness of data, ad hoc reporting and the use of source documents for inputting to the system. In a major departure from the current system's practice of monthly update and preformatted reports, the new GAS will update daily all of the general ledger accounts and provide managers with an on-line query capability to the data base at the Project, SOC, ORN level. The concept requires that the results of transactions processed as of the close of business one day be available for query by Agency managers at the beginning of business the next day. These capabilities will reduce the need to maintain manual records. GAS can also provide off-line queries and produce ad hoc reports which are presently compiled manually. Ad hoc reports can be produced within four to 24 hours.

Forms have been designed to permit the use of source documents in lieu of coding sheets, whenever possible, for keying input of data into the system. In addition to relieving the user of transcribing data from a source document to a coding sheet, this capability obviously provides an advantage in elimination of coding errors.

The new system will also generate posting vouchers, currently prepared manually, from the Payroll (APS) and Logistics (ICS) systems, and will automate certain functions, such as closing entries on a daily cycle, that are currently prepared monthly on a manual basis.

The advantages of GAS in both the accounting and Agency-wide resource management functions—validation and rejection of erroneous data; daily update of all ledgers; single entry input using transaction codes; minimal report lag; on-line query capability; ad hoc requests within 24 hours and an expanded data base that will provide more data for managers than any previous system—certainly warrant the air of excitement permeating OF these days.

secret

Directorate of Administration

secret

october 1976

dda exchange

confidential

Approved For Release 2002/01/08 : CIA-RDP86-00114R000100150003-1

"... just as it is more exciting to build a new boat than to scrape away the barnacles year after year, there is a tendency to give higher priority to a new dramatic policy initiative than to consider the programs we already have to see how they can be improved—to scrape away the 'barnacles,' that build up over time around almost any program or agency."

President Ford

Memorandum for D/OMB dated July 24, 1976, that inaugurates the Presidential Management Initiatives program in the Federal Government.

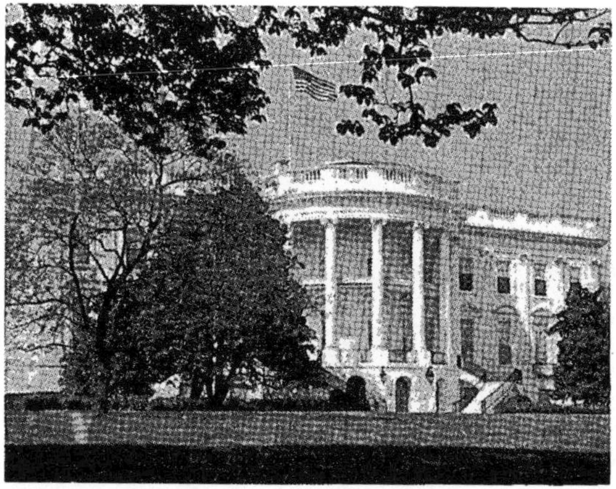

dda exchange

A publication designed to furnish a medium for the exchange of ideas, concepts, information, and techniques that are of common interest to the personnel who are engaged in resource management in the Directorate of Administration.

NATIONAL SECURITY INFORMATION

Unauthorized Disclosure Subject to Criminal Sanctions

staff

SENIOR EDITORS		
Jerry Booth	OS	5311
Kent Cargile	OP	7165
Jean DeBlois	OC	8-8366
Hazel Harrison	OL	8-8131
Kent Schott	OF	2767
Jerry Starliper	ODP	6979
Glenn Steele	OMS	7724
Wendell Tewell	OTR	3107
ASSOCIATE EDITORS		
Parker Archibald	CMO-DDA	4142
Hal Bean	AI-DDA	5003
Bob Zunzer	EO-DDA	6535
MANAGING EDITOR		
Helen Vigness	M&AS-DDA	5226
ADMINISTRATIVE ASSOCIATE		
Karen Foley	EEO-DDA	7726

index

comment

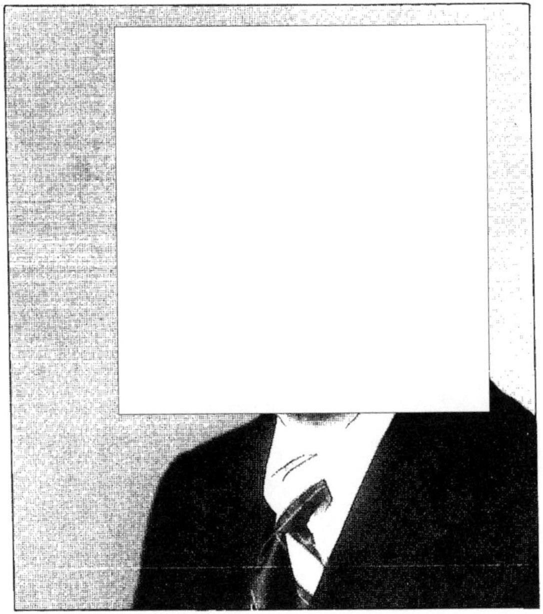

Without a doubt, these last two years have been the most traumatic in the Agency's history. Beginning with Watergate and the subsequent publication of the Seymour Hersh article in *The New York Times* on 22 December 1974, we have undergone experiences which could have had us hanging on the ropes awaiting the proverbial knock-out blow. Through persistance, dedication and dogged determination, we hung on, managed to weather the storm, and now we should be able to get back to our normal day-to-day activities. Unfortunately, however, "day-to-day activities" now are different and include more work than they did two years ago. For example, today we have the Freedom of Information and Privacy Acts to cope with, as well as the resultant new directives or executive orders, all of which add new dimensions and challenges to our way of life. Just this week, I initialed off on a report which indicated that

Michael J. Malanick
Associate Deputy Director
for Administration

we had a backlog of 1207 unanswered FOIA requests and, considering the fact that it takes about an average of two months to reply to one request, it's easy to see that the backlog will be with us for some time unless some relief comes along. Then too, each time a story about the Agency appears in the press, you can bet your bottom dollar it will be followed by FOIA requests. Furthermore, some changes in public attitudes have brought with them a movement to change our security policies and practices and, while many of them could be for the better, some may represent a radical difference from what we would like to see. The unwanted notoriety we have experienced has precipitated a closer examination of our relationships with other elements of the Government at the federal, state and municipal level. Changes in senior management have brought in new perceptions and concepts and we're being asked to explain or reexamine our personnel policies and practices. With the new oversight bodies in the Congress and heightened interest by the House Appropriations Committee, we are obviously going to have to justify more than ever before the need for each and every program we hope to undertake and each expenditure we want to make. All of the above are just a few of the challenges we will face not only in this coming year but in all those that follow. But just as we survived three intensive investigations and have received much harsh public criticism, we can and will continue to stand tall in the Community, thanks to the efforts of people such as you who are in this Directorate. (Unclassified)

vol. 1, no. 3

The DDA . . . 1977

Happy New Year!

October 1 marks the beginning of our fiscal year.

Just as you and I begin the new calendar year with resolutions, we also begin the new fiscal year with Directorate resolutions.

We, in the Directorate of Administration, resolve to:

Revise, as required, and reissue under current date all Headquarters Regulations (HR's) by 31 December 1977.

Some regulations no longer provide current guidance or may be suspect because of their very age. The update will attest to Agency users and to external reviewers the currency of these Agency policy statements.

Extend the overseas security program by 30 September 1977 to include personal, residential, and facility protection.

Assassinations, robberies, riots, terrorist actions, kidnappings—all present a real and present danger to our fellow employees overseas. Their safety dictates extension of the program from primary focus on our installations to encompass the personal security of our employees and dependents in their homes, travel to and from work, etc.

Develop and implement by 30 September 1977 a program for 30-year mandatory declassification of records.

In September 1977 the Agency will celebrate its 30th birthday. The birthday also marks the beginning date when CIA records fall within the purview of the 30-year mandatory declassification law.

Install automated field terminal (AFT) communication systems in [redacted] *field stations by 30 September 1977.*

Communications is the vital link with our overseas stations and the life blood of intelligence. The objective denotes our commitment to maintenance of a communications system equal to the demands levied on it and to expectations of excellence.

Produce a booklet during FY 1977 describing information that is available through the Office of Personnel's Statistical Reporting Branch.

We recognize that managers do "need to know." The booklet will provide a means for our managers to optimize use of information being accumulated for their purposes.

Develop a plan for electronic funds transfer for employees payrolled openly as CIA and for CIARDS annuitants.

This is one more step in our efforts toward improving efficiency through capitalizing on use of the computer's capability for handling information.

Put into operation by April 1981 a reliable and expandable on-line data processing system (SAFE) to facilitate the intelligence analysts' access to and use of intelligence data.

SAFE is a major, multi-million dollar project in which Congress, OMB, and senior Agency officals are interested. Creation of the system will require a high degree of technical and managerial skills and close coordination between components in DDA and DDI.

25X1

Los Angeles audit office of CSAD, for instance, has a liaison arrangement with the DCAA Regional Director of that area. In order to insure that the Government pays fair and reasonable prices for desired quality, information is passed between DCAA and CSAD. In pursuit of this goal the relationship has been beneficial to both organizations.

The Agency's needs are so varied that it finds itself doing business with organizations as small as one person and as large as multi-national corporations. As an illustration of this diversity, CSAD as of 1 July 1976 is auditing about 2,200 contracts placed with 380 contractors.

The Proprietary Systems Branch (PSB) is concerned with Agency owned or controlled commercial type activities. PSB concurs for the Director of Finance in Administrative and Liquidation Plans and has custody of protective documents such as stock certificates, notes, assignments, etc. The branch approves and/or develops accounting systems for proprietaries and performs consultations on accounting and proprietary matters. It performs certifications of proprietary financial transactions and analyzes, reconciles and processes financial statements issued by the proprietaries. PSB also maintains the General Ledger and accounting records for the Voluntary Investment Plan and issues financial and statistical reports. It also gives financial advice and assistance to and prepares tax returns for non-appropriated fund activities, such as EAA and GEHA. (Unclassified)

25X1

communications

25X1

PLANNING FOR A CRISIS: THE OC EMERGENCY DESTRUCTION PROGRAM

D.K. Aitken

Fast-breaking events which lead to the evacuation of the official American presence in the field present a variety of problems to OC. The 1967 Middle East crisis, the Vietnam evacuation, and the current situation in

Lebanon are examples of cases where it is critically important to maintain secure communications up until the last possible moment before evacuation. The example of Beirut proves that there may be no way of knowing just how long a crisis situation will last.

Maintaining a communications capability in the face of imminent evacuation means a certain amount of material and equipment must remain functional up until the actual moment of departure, and must be quickly and completely destroyed at the proper time. A sound destruction program is the key to planning for communications in such a situation.

As part of its emergency planning, OC has developed a worldwide emergency destruction program to ensure the timely and systematic safehavening and/or destruction of classified cryptographic material and equipment, and classified files. The objectives of the program can usually be met without severely affecting OC's primary functions of providing essential, secure communications in a crisis.

OS has helped OC develop this program by providing basic guidelines which OC has adapted to its own unique communications role. Both components together periodically review the procedures in the program to determine if they should be revised or updated.

Basic to this destruction program is an emergency destruction plan, and every OC facility overseas has one. Each plan varies according to local conditions and circumstances, since experience has shown the plan must be tailored to fit the post to be effective. Every professional and nonprofessional communicator is thoroughly indoctrinated in emergency planning, and is trained in the use of such destruction devices and techniques as incinerators, desintegrators and sodium nitrate.

The emergency destruction plans are divided into three phases. The three phases permit the amount of classified holdings to be gradually reduced as the threat to the security and tenability of the OC facility escalates. Because of the unique OC requirement to maintain secure communications, the three phases differ from the emergency destruction routine of other Agency components at the post. These three phases have been successfully completed in time periods ranging from twenty minutes to a number of weeks, depending upon the amount of classified material and equipment to be destroyed and the situation. Before any phase of the plan may be implemented, authorization must be granted by the senior Agency official present at the post. The plan defines the duties and responsibilities in enough detail to maintain full operational effectiveness under each action phase.

All OC personnel review the emergency destruction plan upon arrival at the OC facility and, at a minimum, semiannually thereafter. A clear understanding of the intent of the emergency destruction plan is vital. OC and its overseas representatives also make a concerted effort to ensure that the plan is an integral part of the post's E&E plan approved by the principal officer. In part, this coordination is intended to ensure that adequate emergency destruction de-

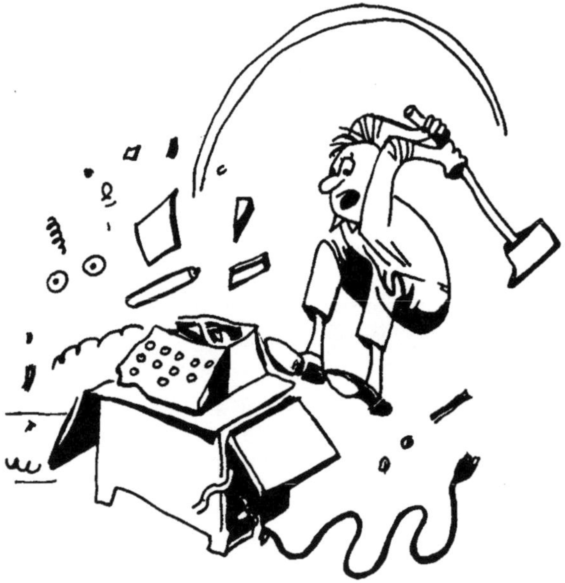

vices and emergency power for their operation will be available when needed.

OC's major assets in the emergency destruction program are its personnel in the field. While there is no sure formula for predicting an individual's action or reactions during an emergency, OC personnel have proved remarkably cool under the pressure of a sudden or prolonged crisis. Over the past ten years, many OC personnel have had occasion to use their emergency destruction plans with no known serious compromise of classified material or equipment.

Emergency destruction planning is a constant process and experience teaches many lessons. As the need arises, OC reviews and amends its emergency destruction program to ensure that it is the best possible in the face of ever changing world conditions. (Unclassified)

data processing

Presidential Management Initiatives- Efficiency Evaluation Study for Minicomputers

Under the Presidential Management Initiatives program the Agency was asked to identify to the Office of Management and Budget ten efficiency evaluations that could be completed before the end of FY 1977. Efficiency evaluations focus on a given activity to determine if there are ways of achieving cost savings, or a more efficient approach to providing a service, or a less burdensome way of achieving program objectives.

One such efficiency evaluation proposed by the Office of Data Processing and subsequently selected by the Comptroller for submission to OMB was an on-going study to determine if an information storage and retrieval application could be performed more efficiently by a standalone minicomputer than by the large scale multi-application computer systems of ODP. This study is an important step in a continuing program in ODP to define the role of minicomputers in the Agency.

Currently, large scale computer systems are used by ODP to provide computer services to a wide range of applications and users throughout the Agency. Many of these can be classified as information storage and retrieval applications. Information storage and retrieval systems have much commonality in the functions that are performed and the ADP techniques that are used to accomplish these functions. When large centralized computers are used for these applications, service to customers is affected by competition among the customers for computer resources, interaction among applications which can slow down response time to one or more users, and occasional system outages. In this study ODP has selected an appropriate application involving a data base containing information on Special Clearances. Data will be converted for use on a minicomputer, programs will be prepared, and operational tests will be performed and evaluated to determine if the minicomputer can provide greater reliability (i.e., less downtime from system failure) and better response time for storage and retrieval functions at less cost.

ODP expects to complete this study by January 1977. (Unclassified)

training

THE AGENCY LANGUAGE PROBLEM AND TOTAL IMMERSION TRAINING

[redacted]

The Agency is losing a high percentage of its foreign language skills through retirements. Today only 54 percent of the universities and colleges in the United States require foreign language as a degree requirement, and young officers entering the Agency are bringing fewer foreign language skills with them. One of the methods now used in OTR to help stop the erosion of our language skills is total immersion training, also referred to as language houses.

These programs, conducted at the [redacted] are limited to 12 students. They live together in a residential setting for a four-week period with four or more native-speaking instructors. The foreign language only is spoken around the clock, making the training stressful for student and instructor alike. In addition to the native-speaker, Agency officers with fluency in the target language and with specialized knowledge also visit as lecturers and role-players to insure that the training is oriented to clandestine operations work. The programs are conducted in close coordination with the operating components; last year's Russian total immersion program was a joint enterprise of OTR and the Soviet East Europe Division.

To date, 100 Agency officers have participated in language houses. Fifty percent of the officers who began the program with an elementary 2 to 2+ speaking proficiency have reached the professional 3 level or better; 70 percent of the officers have improved their language skills at least one-half level; all have developed confidence in dealing with operational problems, which are emphasized.

Those who benefit most from the instruction are officers with a 2 or 2+ speaking

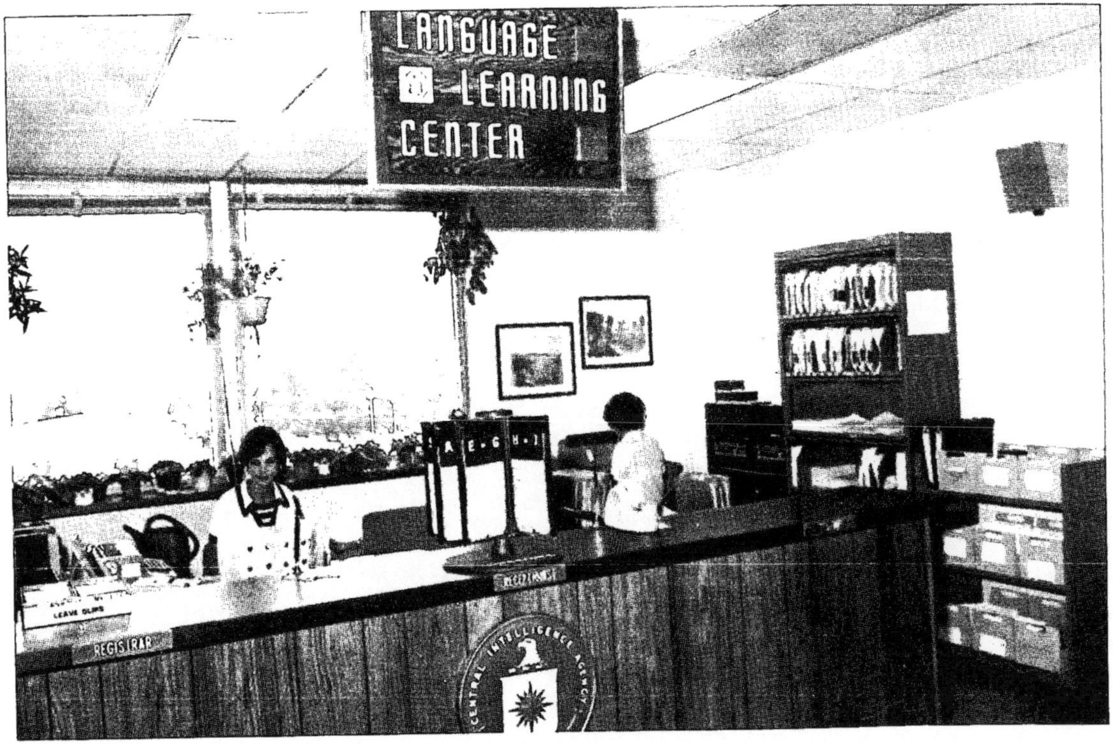
LANGUAGE
LEARNING
CENTER
LEAVE SLIPS
REGISTRAR
CENTRAL INTELLIGENCE AGENCY

proficiency and are designated for overseas assignment shortly after the course. These officers clearly have the proper background and motivation to obtain maximum benefit from the training, and leave the course with the necessary preparation to conduct Agency business abroad. Our language houses do not produce miracles or native speakers, but they do provide a sound approach to the difficult problem of enabling officers with a good foundation to reach professional competency.

In FY 1977 the Language Learning Center will offer total immersion courses in Chinese, French, German, Spanish and Russian. With careful student selection, these programs are making a major contribution to offsetting dwindling Agency language skills at the professional level. (Unclassified)

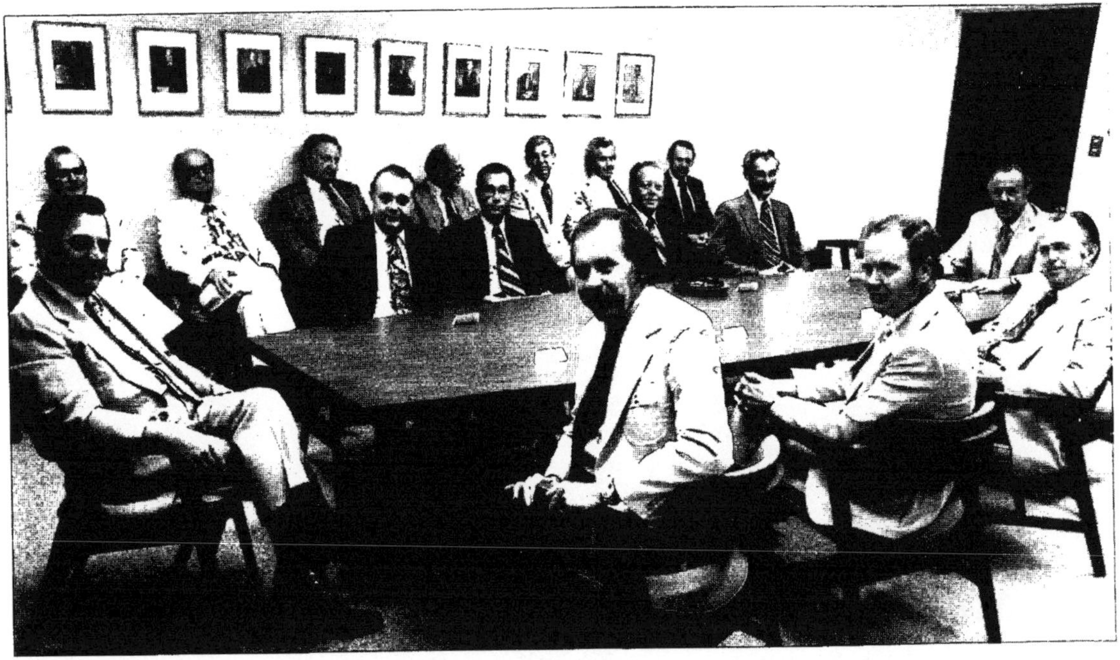

innovation

DDA PERSONNEL ROTATION PROGRAM

[redacted] *CMO/DDA*

Agency management has long been concerned about the multi-discipline development of Agency officers ultimately capable of assuming the most senior positions such as Staff and Division Chief, Office Director and Deputies and Associate Deputies at the Directorate level. It has been generally recognized that those individuals possessing the broadest possible backgrounds will be best qualified to assume these high level executive positions in the Agency of the future.

Recognizing the need for such development in the Directorate of Administration and because of our particularly diverse functions, the Deputy Director for Administration, last May, announced the establishment of the senior DDA Personnel Rotation Program. The pilot phase of this effort was designed to operate on a limited basis but as experience is gained its expansion is envisioned.

Each DDA Office Director (except Director of Medical Services) was asked to identify at least one position at the GS-15/16 level which could be staffed by an officer from another sub-group. Further, at least two officers (GS-14/15) from each sub-group were to be nominated as candidates for rotation. Each Office was asked to ensure that all qualified employees were considered for participation.

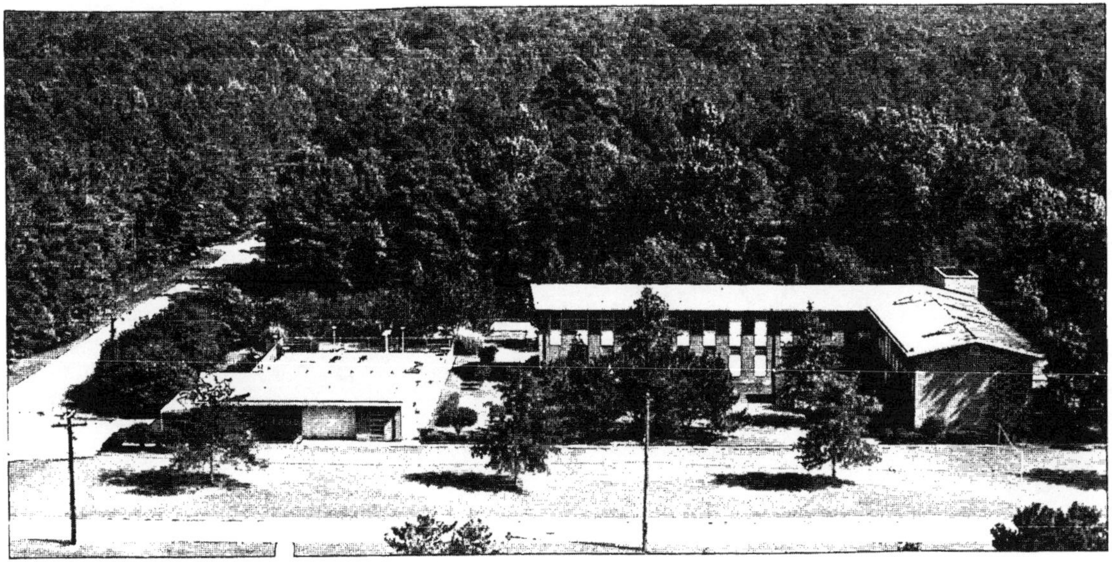

The total sleeping capacity of the LAUREL Building consists of 34 single bedroom and 13 single bed/sitting room duplex accommodations. There is also a VIP bedroom suite and, if required, the seminar-study area can be converted into an additional VIP accommodation. Conference rooms are located on both the first and second floors, and each can conveniently accommodate up to 24 people. A 25-meter swimming pool with diving boards is located adjacent to the building and is available for use on the "buddy" system.

The LAUREL Conference Building is located at the rear of the Public Works Building, just off Raccoon Road. It is more convenient to the Main Gate than most other STC facilities, but transportation is needed to get to the Mess Hall. Bus service and other transportation can be provided when required.

The LAUREL Conference Building has already been used by small working groups who have found its relative isolation highly conducive to work and its accommodations comfortable and pleasant. (Unclassified)

definition

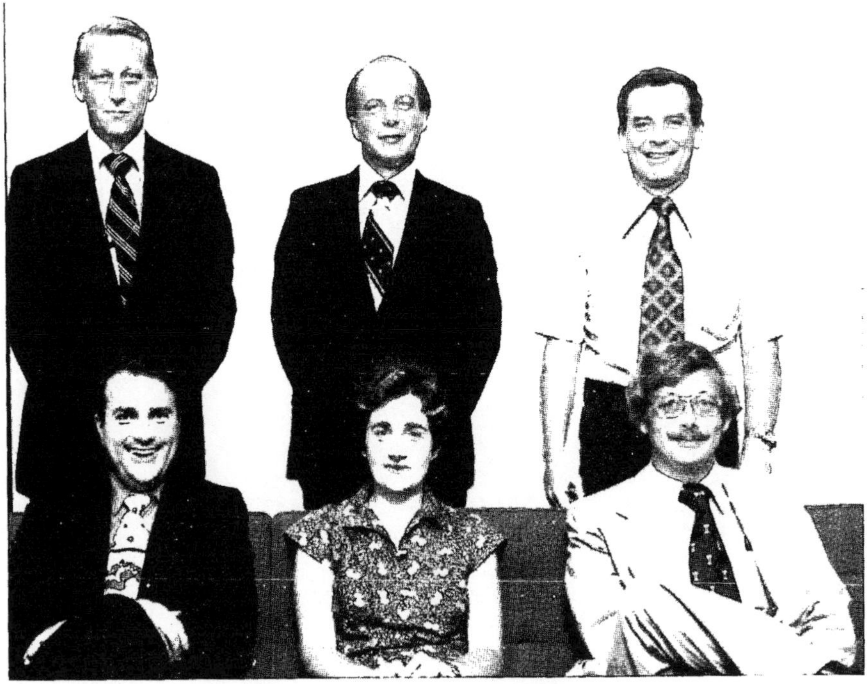

Front row: Jeff Willis, Doris Feinsilber, Bob Thall; Back: Wayne Edgington, Bill Golder, Jack Smith; Not present: Jim Gatton, Art Choate, Gail Thomson

features

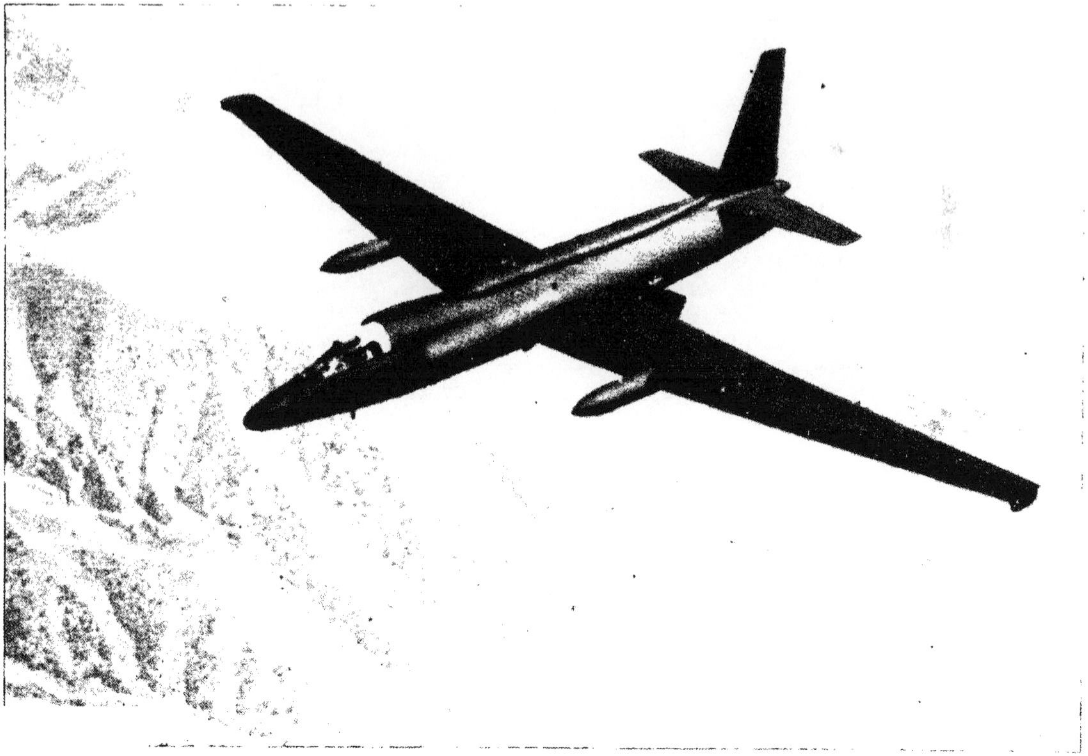

SWINE FLU VACCINE—A SHOT IN THE DARK?

[redacted], *M.D., OMS*

Just over 250 years ago, Calvinist theologian Cotton Mather learned from his African slave, Onesimus (who was "a pretty Intelligent Fellow"), that he once "had undergone an Operation, which had given him something of the Small-Pox, and would forever preserve him from it . . ." The operation involved inoculation with fresh, virulent pustular material from an active case of smallpox, and the idea was not a winning one in Boston. The very concept was viewed as dangerous, irreligious, and probably criminal.

The Reverend Mather nonetheless thought the idea worth a trial, but managed to convince only a single physician, one Zabdiel Boylston, to try "the New Method." When the next epidemic swept through Boston, in the fall of 1721, Boylston inoculated some 242 people. Nearly 50% of the population of Boston (then about 12,000) contracted smallpox that year, and of those nearly 15% died. Among the inoculated group, deaths totalled only 2%.

Thus began the practice of immunization in America. In the following three centuries, vaccines have been developed against some of the most devastating diseases known to man—after smallpox (and its more modern derivative, "vaccination" with cowpox), came vaccines for rabies, typhoid fever, cholera, plague, tuberculosis, diphtheria, tetanus, pneumonia, yellow fever, typhus, whooping cough, poliomyelitis, mumps, measles, rubella . . . and now swine flu. Although not all were totally successful, or safe, collectively they represent one of the most important accomplishments in the history of medicine.

Despite the early successes of immunization programs, widespread public—and medical—opposition continued. Heated controversy accompanied the use of inoculation throughout the eighteenth century. It was said to *cause* smallpox in healthy people (it did!), start epidemics (probably true), and kill (one of every 50 inoculated died) or disfigure its victims. In short, it was considered by many too dangerous to use regardless of the alternatives. Even the introduction of cowpox vaccination in 1796, a much safer procedure than inoculation, induced only a temporary lull in what shortly became a major anti-vaccination crusade. While the dangers of immunization had decreased, the successes of vaccination had reduced even further the risk of contracting the disease.

By 1870, apathy and antipathy were so widespread that most Americans were completely unprotected against smallpox. Predictably, it shortly returned in force, and smallpox epidemics periodically swept the United States well into the twentieth century. Only within the past few decades has smallpox truly been banished from America, as well as most of the world. Ironically, for most Americans vaccination today in fact does pose a greater threat than does smallpox itself.

The controversy surrounding immunization programs is based on a delicate balance that weighs the risks to individuals and society from a given illness against the risks inherent in a preventative vaccine. At one time, such decisions were relatively easy. Epidemics of diphtheria killed over 50% of infected children in some areas of colonial America; among the general population, smallpox routinely took 10-20% to the grave; and the less frequent, but more terrifying yellow fever epidemics occasionally had fatality rates approaching 50%.

A vaccine didn't have to be very safe to beat these odds, if it could be delivered in a timely manner. A classic example was the early rabies vaccines, used regularly to combat a disease that was 100% fatal, but itself extracting a very high price in death and paralysis.

By the mid-twentieth century, all this had changed. When the Salk vaccine against poliomyelitis was rushed into production in

1955, and some 365 children contracted polio from defective vaccine, the public and medical outcry was almost unprecedented—even though several million additional doses had been successfully administered without serious complication. Subsequently, the somewhat more effective Sabin oral vaccine was introduced, with a margin of safety considered acceptable—about one significant complication in 4,000,000 doses.

Influenza vaccines have been, in a sense, the black sheep in the history of immunology. Despite being very safe, flu shots have just never caught on. Americans overwhelmingly (and rightfully) have viewed the flu as more a nuisance than a threat, and routine immunization has not been recommended for most healthy adults. Influenza is not without serious risks, however. An estimated 60,000-70,000 Americans died in the pandemic of "Asian flu" in 1957-58, and nearly 30,000 in the more recent "Hong Kong flu" epidemic of 1968-69. Even so, the deaths were almost always due to secondary complications in elderly or otherwise weak or debilitated individuals. Healthy adults and youth were generally only incapacitated for a few days. Consequently, only those in unusually vulnerable conditions, or occupying positions where even a relatively brief illness must be avoided, have routinely received influenza vaccination.

But there are influenzas, and then there are influenzas. The infamous influenza pandemic of 1918 was much less a respector of persons than its modern, relatively toothless grandchildren. With a perverse abandon, this modern plague felled primarily young, healthy adults. Though the overall case fatality rate was only 1 in 200, so widespread was the disease that some 500,000 Americans died from its complications—ten times the American deaths in World War I. Worldwide, there were an estimated 20 million deaths, and in some communities over 10% of the young men succumbed.

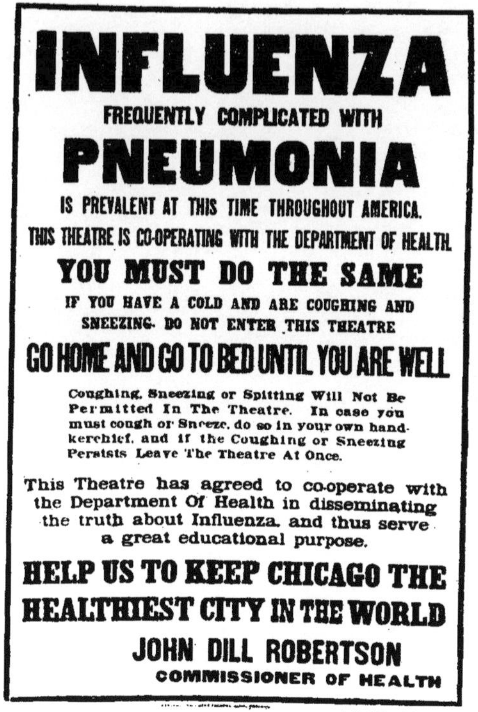

INFLUENZA

FREQUENTLY COMPLICATED WITH

PNEUMONIA

IS PREVALENT AT THIS TIME THROUGHOUT AMERICA.

THIS THEATRE IS CO-OPERATING WITH THE DEPARTMENT OF HEALTH.

YOU MUST DO THE SAME

IF YOU HAVE A COLD AND ARE COUGHING AND SNEEZING. DO NOT ENTER THIS THEATRE

GO HOME AND GO TO BED UNTIL YOU ARE WELL

Coughing, Sneezing or Spitting Will Not Be Permitted In The Theatre. In case you must cough or Sneeze, do so in your own handkerchief, and if the Coughing or Sneezing Persists Leave The Theatre At Once.

This Theatre has agreed to co-operate with the Department Of Health in disseminating the truth about Influenza, and thus serve a great educational purpose.

HELP US TO KEEP CHICAGO THE HEALTHIEST CITY IN THE WORLD

JOHN DILL ROBERTSON

COMMISSIONER OF HEALTH

1918 Poster

It was therefore no mere curiosity when investigators studying an outbreak of flu at Fort Dix, New Jersey, this past February found it to be indistinguishable from "swine" flu. For it was into the pig population that the 1918 strain eventually disappeared, apparently no longer infecting man.

Was it the 1918 strain? Identification techniques fifty years ago were not sophisticated enough to allow an absolute confirmation, but available indicators suggested it was the same. Would it be just as virulent? Possibly not. There was only one fatality among the 500 cases at Fort Dix, and today we are much better able to treat serious complications. Still, it is too early to know for sure. The swine flu (technically the "A/New Jersey strain") did not spread from Fort Dix this past winter; but the 1918 strain probably also had been around a year or more prior to the pandemic. If a new epidemic was about to begin, it would not be until at least the next flu season—late fall and winter, 1976-77.

The decision to undertake a massive, preemptive immunization campaign against a potential, but still hypothetical, epidemic of a dangerous new strain of influenza was therefore made within an extensive historical context. Fortunately, a major problem in the past was largely irrelevant to the current decision. Immunology had come a long way since 1721, and the flu vaccines were very safe—*no* documented fatalities reported in thirty years. The final decision, then, was quickly reduced to weighing the cost in dollars and manpower (and minimal associated malaise) against the likelihood that a serious epidemic would be avoided. A vaccine was available, which at 70% effectiveness, should, if effectively utilized, blunt an epidemic.

But is there going to be an epidemic? In the final analysis, this seemingly central question has become irrelevant. For, how likely does an epidemic have to be before a safe, but expensive, program would be appropriate? One chance in three? In ten? If there was a reasonable risk, and there definitely is, there was no real alternative. (Unclassified)

confidential

april 1977

dda exchange

confidential

Page Denied

Next 1 Page(s) In Document Denied

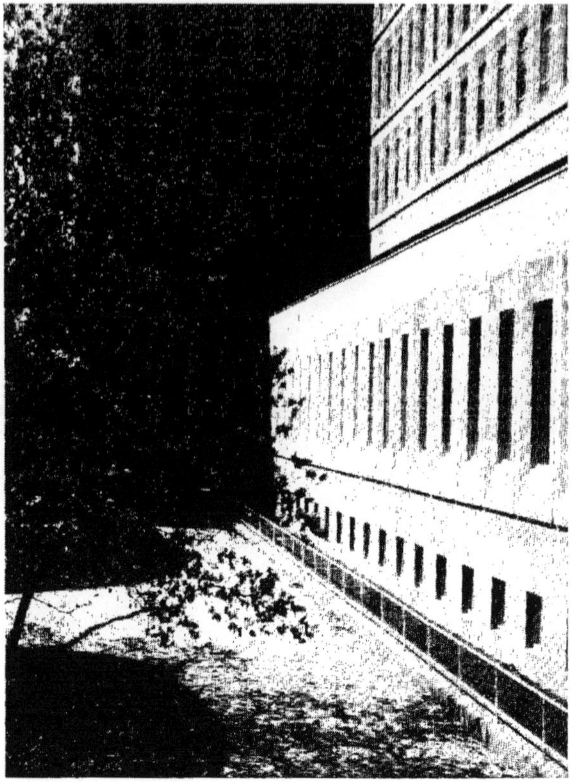

"Coming together is a beginning; keeping together is progress; working together is success."

Henry Ford

help!
see
page 58

dda exchange

A publication designed to furnish a medium for the exchange of ideas, concepts, information, and techniques that are of common interest to the personnel who are engaged in resource management in the Directorate of Administration.

VOLUME 2, NO. 2

NATIONAL SECURITY INFORMATION

Unauthorized Disclosure Subject to Criminal Sanctions

Classified by 000288
Exempt from General Declassification Schedule
of E.O. 11652, exemption category:
§5B(1), (2), and (3)
Automatically declassified on:
date impossible to determine

25X1

staff

25X1

SENIOR EDITORS

25X1

[redacted]

OS
OP
OC
OMS
OL
OF
ODP
OTR

25X1

25X1

ASSOCIATE EDITORS

[redacted]

CMO-DDA
A-I-DDA
EO-DDA

MANAGING EDITOR

[redacted] M&AS-DDA

ADMINISTRATIVE ASSOCIATE

[redacted] M&AS-DDA

[redacted]

index

comment

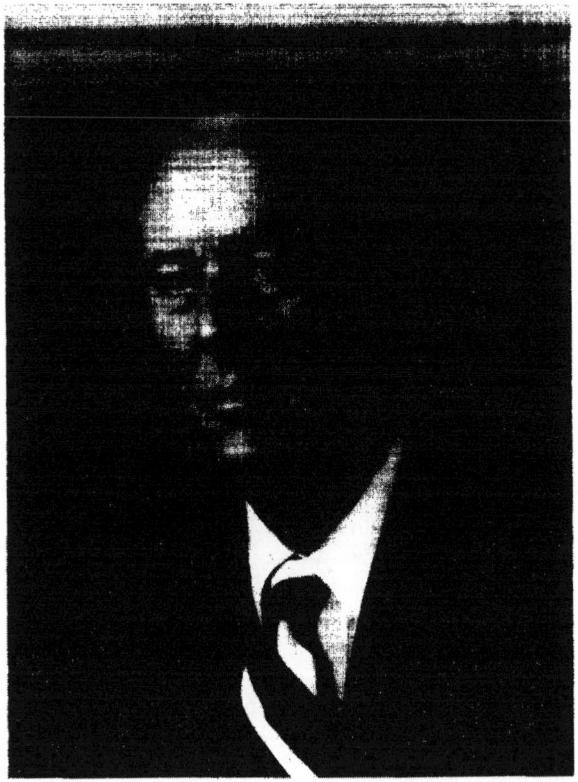

This edition of DDA *Exchange* marks the first anniversary for publication of our Directorate magazine. Tradition dictates a pause, on such an occasion, to assess our present state and prospects for the future. Since the Reader Survey will do that for DDA *Exchange,* this Comment will address the present state and future prospects for the Directorate.

The Directorate of Administration is alive and well—it is full of life. All the vital signs are good. It is functioning; it is growing—that is, maturing; it is responding to challenge; and it is building foundations for the future. The articles in this issue of DDA *Exchange* themselves bear witness to the vitality of the Directorate.

Read about the couriers—the "conveyors" of the intelligence product from its raw to finished stage. Read the story of the [redacted] that teaches "how to" combat hostile audio surveillance. Re-

25X1 25X1

John F. Blake, DD/A

Page Denied

forum

several areas for improvement or innovation; one identified need was for an orientation course for new employees in the technical and office-worker fields. OTR has since begun such a course. On the whole, Agency managers registered a vote of confidence in the Agency's training program with the task force.

Another measure comes from an in-depth review of all Agency training activities by a three-man investigating team from the House Appropriations Committee's staff. The team has recently completed its study over a six-month period. Their findings are not available to the Agency until the Appropriations Committee has reviewed their report. However, the team, which includes one member who was the director of training of another major government organization until his retirement in August 1975, concluded that the Agency has a first-rate training program.

Finally, the Agency rank and file have indicated, in the Agency personnel management survey published last December, that they are satisfied with the training they obtain and believe they have adequately utilized it in better performance in their jobs. (UNCLASSIFIED)

logistics

PROFILE: THE COURIERS

The product of this Agency is essentially information. Raw data is received from a multitude of sources in many forms which must be transformed into useful information for distribution to our consumers. The conveyors of that product, from its raw materials form through its production stages to the consumer, are the Agency couriers. A comprehensive, graphic presentation depicting that activity would resemble a bowl of spaghetti.

The courier shop is a busy place responding to the routine, the ad hoc, and the priority. Packages must be x-rayed for bombs, newspapers must be delivered early, and the telephone rings constantly.

The couriers drive in excess of half a million miles a year, walk thousands of miles, deliver millions of pieces of correspondence and equipment weighing thousands of tons. They must know every major Federal building in the area and its idiosyn- [redacted] and access clearances and must know who is authorized to receive each piece of mail they carry and the procedures required to transmit it. The intelligence community is as familiar to them as the back of their hand, and they list the offices of the Secretaries of State and Defense and the President of the United States among their multitude of customers.

Hundreds of employees have entered on duty through the Mail and Courier Branch. A new employee assigned to the branch can quickly become productive while adjusting to a new situation and life style. They also get a good look at the Agency, its functions, offices, and personnel. Proper supervision and development for the new, young employee is essential.

Those who choose to remain, the journeymen, are the backbone of the operation. They may work for days without the presence of a supervisor. They live as close as [redacted]

25X1

Page Denied

Page Denied

25X1

medical services

PSYCHOLOGICAL TESTS

[redacted] Ph.D., OMS

For over twenty years, the results of tests given by Psychological Services Staff to applicants and employees, and especially the Professional Test Battery (PATB and PETB), have played some role in personnel decisions affecting the individuals tested. We are frequently asked: (a) how large a role? (b) how useful? (c) how valid? The answers, in short, are respectively: (a) don't know; (b) evidently, quite useful; and (c) demonstrably, quite valid.

The first question, that of the impact of the test battery, is the hardest to answer; the answer lies in the ways in which Agency components utilize the test results. To the credit of the staff psychologists and consultants who established the testing program, no assumptions were made concerning what the levels of abilities, the desirable personal traits and attitudes, or the indicated interests of the Agency professional ought to be. Instead, three other assumptions governed. The first was that the diversity of professional jobs within the Agency accommodated such a wide range of interests, abilities, and styles that selection of anyone's stereotypical ideal was bound to be off base. The second was that those persons closest to the job—the immediate supervisors and the personnel officers in the component concerned—were better able to make selection and assignment decisions than were persons far removed from the target job. The third assumption was that the best service which such a psychological testing service could provide to the selection and assignment process was that of giving a descriptive picture of the candidate, providing information on general abilities, personality traits, attitudes, and interests which those closest to the job could translate into strengths and liabilities for the position as they see it. The line of reasoning giving rise to the testing program was that it should not be one of setting cut-off scores or minimum standards but one of providing management information about the candidate which could not be derived from other sources—including interviews. Thus the typical PATB report provides a description of the individual—not scores or pass-fail decisions, but a narrative description of attitudes and interests, style and abilities. The weight given to such reports varies greatly. Some of the many factors in addition to the test report which enter into the decision process are the amount, detail, and quality of other information the decision maker has about the candidate, the extent to which the psychological test report is congruent with the other information, and the experience and attitudes of the decision maker with respect to the use of test reports. It is in those instances where test results appear to be inconsistent with academic records or job history that the psychological tests demonstrate their greatest utility. Through raising questions which force the decision maker to seek additional information, such as interview reports, a close evaluation of transcripts, examination of previous work performed by the candidate, or reports from references, the decision maker can make a more accurate appraisal of the true potential offered by the candidate.

The second question, how useful is the test data, is easier to answer. The utility of the tests is underscored by the insistence of Agency managers that test results should be available at the earliest stages of applicant consideration and by the extremely wide range of Agency components requesting test reports. The test data is most useful when little is known about the candidate. In instances where there is a limited work history or where the candidate's training and experience are in areas other than that for which he/she is being considered, the test report can help reduce uncertainty about the match between the individual and the requirements of the position. Where there is a history of successful performance in assignments similar to those of the "target" assignment, the test report, obviously, provides less novel information to the decision maker.

The third question concerns the validity of the test battery, the degree to which it measures or predicts that which it is intended to predict. PSS has traditionally taken the position that research indicating the relationship between test scores and job performance is imperative. The ultimate ideal of testing is to develop a series of prediction equations which accurately forecast the candidate's potential for success in any of the wide range of Agency job categories for which he/she is likely to be considered. There are numerous obstacles to reaching this ideal, but PSS continually conducts research studies on the validity of the Professional Test Battery as it relates to specific Agency jobs. The validity research over the years has added significantly to the predictive utility of the tests, and test validation and job performance research constitute a major part of PSS research activities.

Psychological test reports, then, constitute another tool which can be used by those who make selection and assignment decisions. The reports provide information which is usually unavailable from other sources. The description of the candidate as presented in the test report is information which the decisionmaker uses in conjunction with other information about the individual. Test reports are used in decision making but do not constitute the sole basis upon which decisions are made. (UNCLASSIFIED)

in conclusion

ABOUT THE READER SURVEY

Since publication of the first issue of *Exchange,* one year ago, its Editors have received numerous comments concerning its design, its content and its usefulness. Although each subsequent issue spurred more comments and suggestions, the informal nature of the feedback did not easily lend itself to analysis. The tear-out questionnaire included with this issue was designed toward this end. It seeks to elicit reader opinion on the effectiveness of *Exchange* and several aspects of its characteristics. Additionally, the responses will help the editors in planning for future editions or direct the content of the magazine toward areas of greatest interest.

The preparation of the questionnaire was in itself a learning experience, and one from which our readers might benefit if they are someday faced with developing a survey of this type. As with any project, we began with a goal: to determine whether or not *Exchange* is effectively accomplishing its purpose of providing a medium for the exchange of information which is of interest to DDA personnel. We also sought the readership's opinion of the quality of *Exchange* and their suggestions for improving it. To provide a basis for categorizing the responses, general demographic data consisting of the reader's general grade category and Office of assignment was included in the questionnaire—the former to provide data relative to perceptions and levels of interest in this communication form among grade categories; the latter to provide information to assist the Senior Editor in each DDA Office.

At an early stage in the process, Psychological Services Staff (OMS/PSS) was consulted for guidance on the framing of the survey form. Included in their advice was the caveat: keep the survey short and the wording brief, unambiguous and simple. PSS also provided us with several examples of previous Agency surveys which we found quite helpful. During the four iterations of survey development which followed, the questions and response choices were tested by M&AS staffers, coordinated with each of the Senior Editors and Associate Editors, and reviewed and discussed in their penultimate form with [redacted]MS/PSS.

Along the way, various speculations were proffered as to which groups might or might not respond to the questionnaire. (Some thought that the higher graded readers were more apt to complete the questionnaire; others felt the lower graded readers would. One editor saw the negative reader as more likely to respond; another saw the positive reader in this role. etc.) Contrasting opinions notwithstanding, we found unifying elements of sincerity and interest among all persons with whom we came in contact during the process of developing the questionnaire. Every member of the Editorial Board as well as others who offered their advice were sincerely interested in pursuing the questionnaire as a means of gaining information which could provide some measure of its effectiveness, and lead to improving the publication.

Accordingly, the Editorial Staff urges you, the reader, to take a few minutes, reflect on your impressions of *Exchange* over the past year, and with candor and sincerity, complete one of the questionnaires contained in this booklet. The completed questionnaire need only be folded, stapled and sent through internal mail to the Managing Editor (Room 7D18, Headquarters). If there are no questionnaires in your copy of *Exchange*, please call your Senior Editor or call [redacted] on extension [redacted] One will be forwarded immediately. We have established 13 May 1977 as a cut-off day in order to begin our analysis of the responses. But if you cannot meet this date, please mail your response anyway—we're always happy to learn your thoughts. (UNCLASSIFIED)

DDA EXCHANGE READER SURVEY

Each reader of this issue is requested to take a few minutes to answer the following questions. Your responses will help the Editors evaluate the acceptance and usefulness of *Exchange.* Please fold the completed survey form and staple it so the address on the reverse side shows, then forward it through internal mail. *Survey responses should be mailed by 13 May 1977.* Results of the survey will be included in a future issue of Exchange.

Please circle the letter corresponding to the most appropriate answer.

1. How much of *Exchange* do you normally read?
   a) All articles b) Most articles c) An article or two d) Usually don't read it
2. To what degree has *Exchange* increased your understanding of the Directorate?
   a) Very high b) High c) Moderate d) Low
3. How do you rate *Exchange* as a source of information?
   a) Excellent b) Good c) Poor d) Very poor
4. In what ways is this information useful to you? (Circle all which apply.)
   a) As applies to your job or Office activities b) As applies to your career development c) As background information d) Other: ____________
5. Do you feel the average length of the publication is:
   a) Too short b) About right c) Too long
6. Would you prefer that *Exchange* be published:
   a) More frequently b) As is [quarterly] c) Less frequently d) Not at all
7. What is your opinion of the general quality of *Exchange*? (writing style, readability, conveyance of message)
   a) Very high b) High c) Low d) Very low
8. What topics or subject areas do you suggest for future publication?

____

____

secret

january 1978

dda exchange

secret

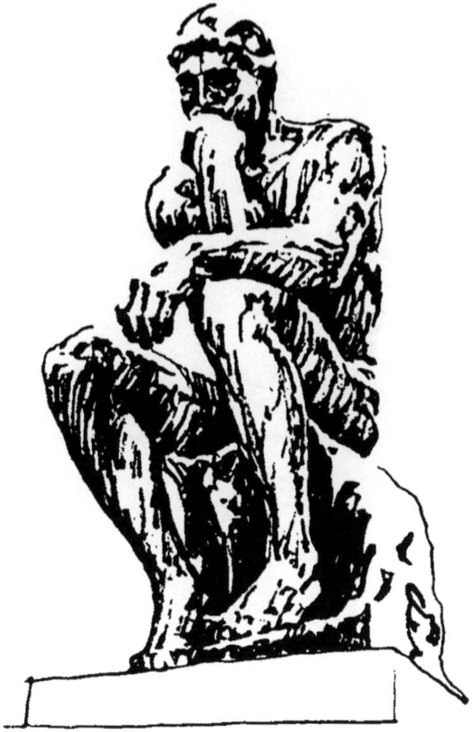

No way of thinking or doing, however ancient, can be trusted without proof.

Henry David Thoreau, *Walden*

dda exchange

A quarterly publication for the exchange among DDA personnel of ideas, concepts, information, and techniques that are of common interest.

NATIONAL SECURITY INFORMATION

Unauthorized Disclosure Subject to Criminal Sanctions

Classified by 000288
Exempt from General Declassification Schedule
of E.O. 11652, exemption category:
Sec 5B(1), (2), and (3)
Automatically declassified on:
date impossible to determine

25X1A

staff

[redacted]

index

VOLUME 3, NO. 1

forum

"ADMINISTRATION IS . . ."

1977 was an especially eventful year for the Agency, for the Directorate, and for each of the offices.

And so, as we turn the calendar with this, the first issue in 1978, we asked each of the Deputy Office Directors the question: "In your opinion, what was the most interesting event in your Office during 1977?"

These are the answers.

25X1A

security

ARRESTS LEAD TO ESPIONAGE CONVICTIONS

[redacted] OS

The arrests of Edwin G. Moore, in December 1976, and of Andrew D. Lee and Christopher J. Boyce in January 1977 on charges stemming from their attempted/actual compromise of CIA classified material have had a resounding impact on OS. Despite the large expenditure of effort, time and money centered on assessing damage done and minimizing recurrences of such actions, one thread common to both cases emerged preeminent: The success of our security program in the past and our hopes for the future depend, most importantly, upon the integrity and reliability of our employees and others who are exposed to sensitive classified material. We have learned that locks, bars, safes and other security hardware can never substitute for that vital human element. (UNCLASSIFIED)

innovation

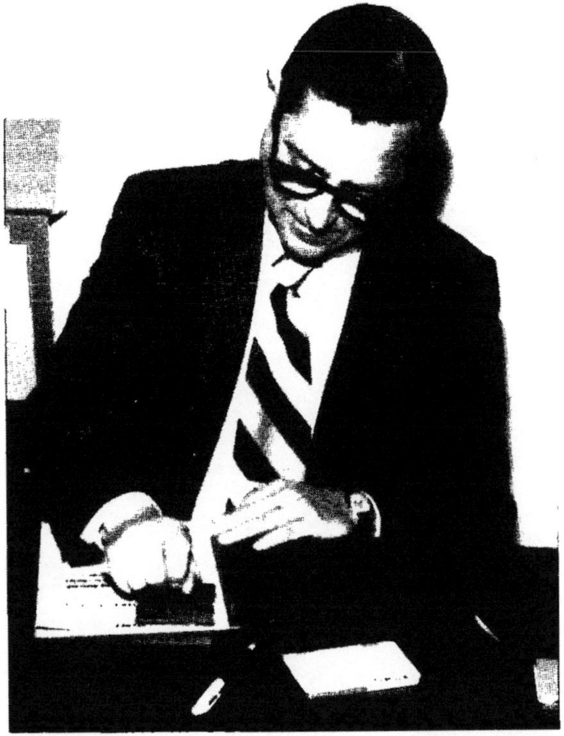

25X1A

DECLASSIFICATION FIRST

Michael J. Malanick, A-DDA, declassifies the first document under the Agency Records Review Program on 18 November 1977.

◀

(C) Directorate Focal Point Officers assigned [redacted]

25X1A

Approved For Release 2002/02/19 : CIA-RDP86-00114R000100130001-5

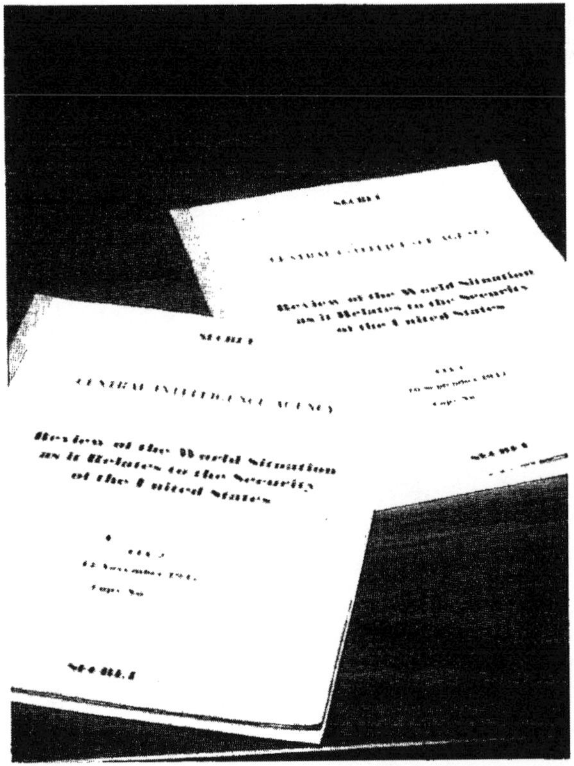

First documents to be declassified under the Agency Records Review Program, produced by the Office of Reports and Estimates.

25X1A

definition

CCCR—WHAT IS IT?

[redacted]OMS

(S) In order to assist in meeting the challenge of terrorist actions throughout the world, OMS has formed the Center for Counterterrorism and Crises Response. The Center provides behavioral science support and guidance to the Agency and the Intelligence Community in the areas of counterterrorism and limited force crises.

(C) Composed of a staff with backgrounds in psychiatry, the behavioral sciences and criminology, CCCR attempts to understand the psychodynamics of individual terrorists and terrorist groups. This involves the collection and analysis of relevant behavioral information from both overt and covert sources.

(U) CCCR also addresses the problems of the victims of terrorism. In this area CCCR develops guidance to be used by potential victims of threats, assassinations, kidnappings, hijackings, etc. Attention is also paid to the management of victims following such trauma. Reentry problems and post-crisis somatic systems are some of the areas under study.

(U) A third major function is the development of crisis management techniques and their application to ongoing crises. Generally this takes the form of providing guidance to the managers and decision makers through appropriate channels.

(S) During the past year CCCR carried out its functions in three areas: data collection, training, and crises management. Management profiles of skyjacking incidents were developed from data provided by airline crews and debriefing of released hostages. Information on the management of terrorist incidents in Europe and Israel was collected through TDY travel to those areas.

(S) In the area of training, CCCR personnel regularly participate in OTR training programs such as the Special Overseas Orienta-

[redacted]

(SECRET)

ZBB IN CIA

[redacted] (MF) O-Compt

(U) Have you seen no potential impact of zero-base budgeting (ZBB) on your job? Is ZBB just another of the short-lived fads such as PPB and MBO brought to you in an ever-changing budget and management alphabet soup? If you answered yes to the above questions, read on and greatly enhance your chance for success and happiness in your Federal career.

What is ZBB?

(U) Zero-base budgeting is a planning, budgeting, and management system that is being used to develop the Fiscal Year 1979 Federal Budget. Though new to the Federal Government in its present form (the US Department of Agriculture made an abortive attempt in the early 1960's at analyzing their budget program from ground zero up), zero-base budgeting has been used by business

secret

april 1978

dda exchange

secret

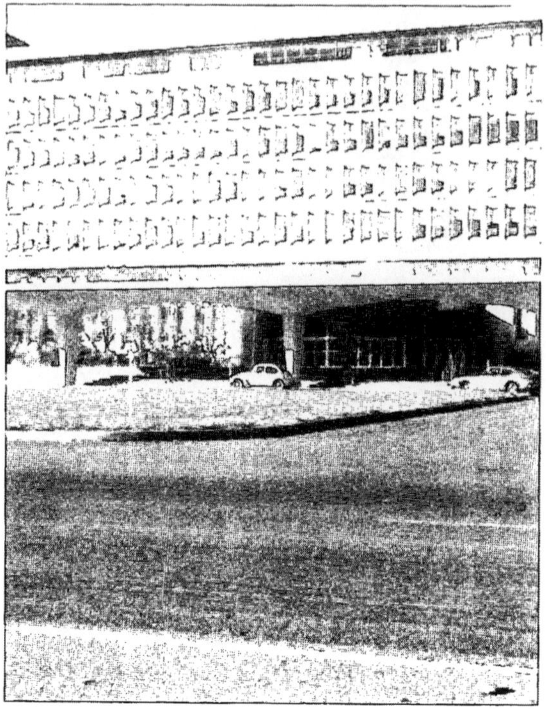

I can say to you with great confidence that I doubt that anywhere else in the business world or in government will you find more dedicated, more capable public servants than in the Central Intelligence Agency and the other associated intelligence organizations in our country. They have an admirable record, and with this I am confident we have the foundation on which to rebuild public confidence which is much deserved.

Stansfield Turner

dda exchange

A quarterly publication for the exchange among DDA personnel of ideas, concepts, information, and techniques that are of common interest.

NATIONAL SECURITY INFORMATION

Unauthorized Disclosure Subject to Criminal Sanctions

Classified by 000288
Exempt from General Declassification Schedule
of E.O. 11652, exemption category:
Sec 5B(1), (2), and (3)
Automatically declassified on:
date impossible to determine

25X1A

staff

SENIOR EDITORS

[redacted]

index

Volume 3, No. 2

forum

"ADMINISTRATION IS . . ."

data processing

TRACKING OUR FOES

[redacted] ODP 25X

(S) Somewhere within a denied territory another test vehicle is launched. And once again the United States attempts to determine the significance of this test by recording the event and analyzing the data. One of the keys to this determination is the intercepted telemetry from this event. With hundreds of similar tests occuring yearly, keeping up with the volume of telemetry and tracking data has become an increasingly difficult task.

25X1A

[redacted]

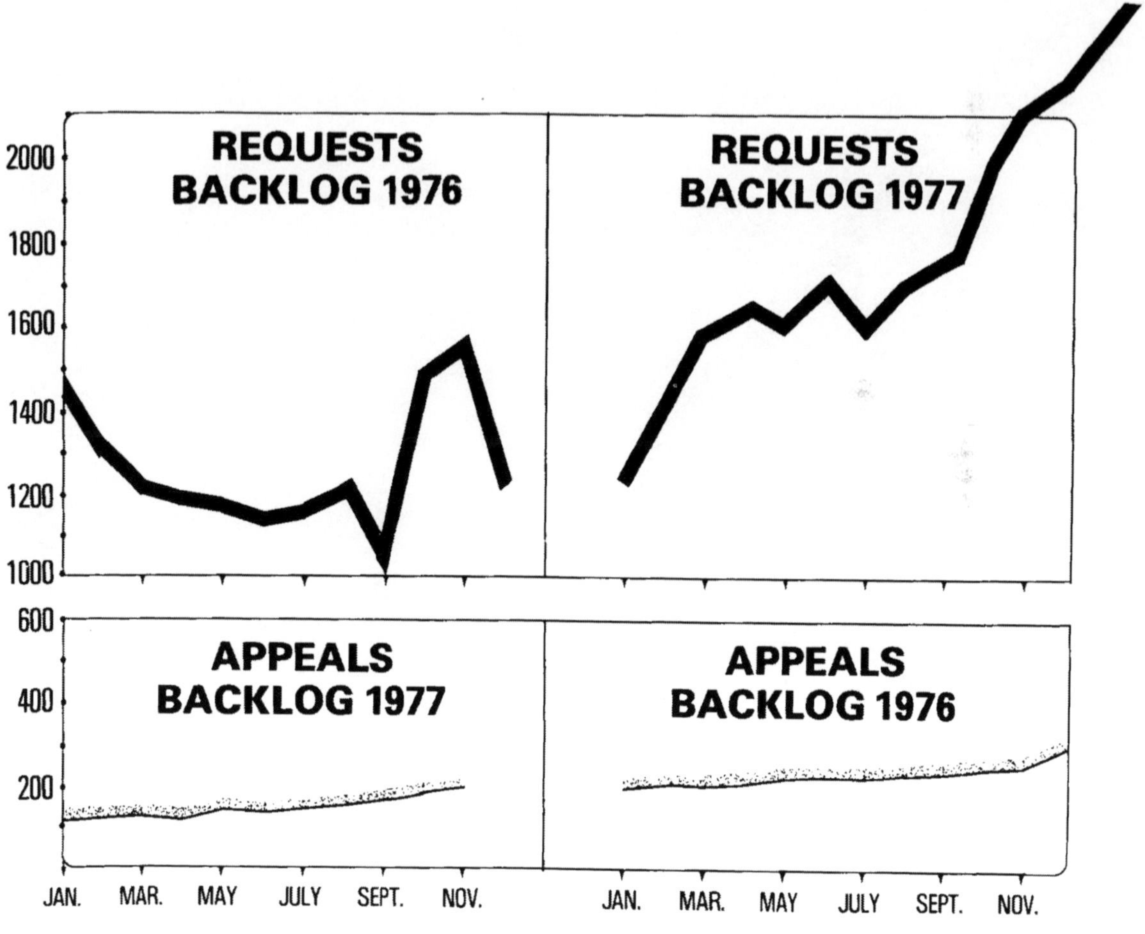
REQUESTS
BACKLOG 1976
REQUESTS
BACKLOG 1977
APPEALS
BACKLOG 1977
APPEALS
BACKLOG 1976
2000
1800
1600
1400
1200
1000
600
400
200
JAN.
MAR.
MAY
JULY
SEPT.
NOV.
JAN.
MAR.
MAY
JULY
SEPT.
NOV.

25X1A

25X1A

communications

THE FIELD COMMUNICATOR—A MOST VALUABLE RESOURCE

[redacted] OC

Many words have been written about CIA communicators and the various jobs they perform in the field. Some call them a necessary evil while others believe that communicators are the greatest thing since Corn Flakes. It probably all depends on individual experiences. If the communicator was the guy who constantly got you out of bed at 2:00 a.m. to read an immediate cable, he would be the bad guy. (Remember, he got up before you, processed this message and then waited around for you to come in.) However, if he copied the message that announced your most recent promotion, or the one that reassigned you to some plush post, then he of course would be the good guy again. It's all relative!

[redacted]

A recent example of the kind of "can do" attitude our communicators have adopted, and a good reason why they are held in such

security

RESIDENTIAL SECURITY

[redacted]OS

Since the death of Mr. Richard Welch, Chief of Station, Athens, in December 1975, OS has been vigorously pursuing a Personnel Protection Program. The Program is designed to protect employees and their families from terrorist and criminal acts that might be aimed against them during their off-duty hours. A big aspect of the Program involves providing advice and guidance on residential security. Recently, the OS Senior Editor requested that an article on this subject be written for publication in DDA Exchange, but from the standpoint of living right here in the United States. This article is offered in response to that request.

Depending upon whose statistics you accept, there are 2.5 or 3 million burglaries each year; one every 10 seconds or one every 15 seconds; and either $400 million or over $500 million in goods stolen each year. The accuracy of these statistics is largely irrelevant, since their value lies only in highlighting the very real fact that burglary is a major crime problem in the United States and one which many of us stand a good chance of encountering at some point in our lifetimes.

Almost everyone either has been the target of a burglary or is acquainted with someone who has been the object of such a criminal act. For example, within the past year, the author's elderly mother was held at gunpoint by three obviously professional thieves while they looted the home where she was babysitting.

Despite experiences of this nature, there is a normal human tendency on the part of most of us to believe that this sort of thing happens to other people and "can't happen here." Until each of us overcomes this mindset and recognizes that we, indeed, can become the target of the burglar, we will not undertake the most elementary precautions to provide for the protection of our homes, our possessions and our families.

The individual should approach the protection of his residence in a systematic fashion, developing an integrated program which contains the various elements which go to make up a completed security system, such as perimeter barriers, lighting, locks, alarms, safehavens and the procedural measures which tie those physical defenses together and make them work. The first step in constructing such a program ought to be a security survey of the residence. This should be accomplished by assessing the defenses of the residence through the eyes of the potential intruder. If you were the burglar, how would you attack your home? Once the vulnerabilities in the defensive posture have been assessed, then you can begin to develop a realistic residential security program.

The primary objective of any burglar is to steal your most valuable possessions and escape with them undetected. The last thing he wants is a confrontation with you, the householder. That is why, contrary to popular belief, a large portion of residential break-ins occurs during daylight hours—the period from 10 a.m. to 4 p.m.—when homes are most likely to be unoccupied. The hours between 6 p.m. and midnight are the second most popular times for the burglar to strike, since this is the period in which most people do their socializing.

Many homes become a target of opportunity because the householder makes himself an inviting target. Thieves will often cruise through neighborhoods looking for tell-tale signs of an unoccupied home in order to line up an easy mark. For this reason, the image or profile which your home projects to the outside world could mean the difference in whether or not you become a target for the burglar. To reduce the chances of being picked as a target in the first place, the householder should refrain from advertising this home as a good place to burglarize by implementing those simple procedural steps which cause a residence to appear to be occupied, or at least make it less obvious that it is unoccupied. These procedures include all the common sense "do's and don't's" which, for all their simplicity, remain valid—keep garage door closed, don't leave messages on door, stop deliveries when on vacation, put lights on and radio on timer, mix up shades and blinds, etc.

Despite these precautions, there is still the chance that your home will become the object upon which the burglar will attempt to ply his trade. You can never completely "burglar proof" your home. Given enough time and the right tools, a determined thief can get into practically any house. The objective of the physical portion of your residential security program should be to build a succession of barriers which make penetration sufficiently difficult and time consuming that the intruder is faced with an unacceptable risk of detection in his attempt to defeat the defenses. There are many easy targets for the burglar; there is no need for him to run the risks involved in taking on a hard target.

Statistics again tell us that, for the most part, burglaries are not committed by professional criminals (although professional "rings or gangs" are certainly active), but in 85 percent of the cases by youthful amateurs under the age of 25. Consequently, in most instances you are not concerned with thwarting a sophisticated attack on your security hardware. Interestingly enough, it has been estimated that between 20 percent and 25 percent of all residential burglaries involved homes which had unlocked doors. So, regardless of the quality of the hardware you might install, it is no good to you unless you use it.

The production and retailing of security hardware and equipment has become a major industry in the United States over the past several years; witness the growth in the residential security hardware departments of such establishments as your local drug and hardware stores. There is a lot of good hardware on the market, and a lot of junk too. Although it is not always necessary to buy the highest priced item, generally "you get what you pay for." There is not the space in this article to engage in a long dissertation on the merits of the various locks and other security equipment which is available for the protection of the doors and windows of your homes. There are available numerous pamphlets, brochures and other publications which treat this subject with great detail. One of the most reliable sources of information on this subject is your local locksmith (and if you are not the "Harry Homeowner" type, he will, of course, be glad to install any equipment you might choose). The "Yellow Pages" of your telephone directory contain numerous listings.

The foregoing comments on security hardware apply equally to residential security alarms, another field which has seen phenomenal growth of late. There is a large variety of residential alarm systems on the market today, although an evaluation of this product is much more difficult for the layman. A number of these systems are not only reliable and affordable, but can be installed relatively easily by the average homeowner.

In addition, a resource for assistance which should not be overlooked is your local police department. The community relations element of the police departments in the Washington, D. C. metropolitan area have crime prevention programs and are eager to assist the residents of their jurisdictions to increase the security of their residences. Some of the departments will present illustrated lectures to organizations; others will conduct security surveys of the individual residence upon request.

(UNCLASSIFIED)

confidential

july 1978

dda exchange

confidential

All human progress, like baseball, involves a certain amount of risk. You can't steal second while keeping one foot on first.

dda exchange

A quarterly publication for the exchange among DDA personnel of ideas, concepts, information, and techniques that are of common interest.

NATIONAL SECURITY INFORMATION

Unauthorized Disclosure Subject to Criminal Sanctions

25X1

25X1A

staff

SENIOR EDITORS

index

Volume 3, No. 3

comment

25X1A

EMPLOYEE GRIEVANCES AND ORGANIZATIONAL EFFECTIVENESS

John H. Waller, Inspector General

[redacted] The health and effectiveness of an organization can be measured by a variety of indicators. At best, the measuring process usually produces results which are open to a number of interpretations. It seems to me, however, that a valid measure of the Agency's health and effectiveness should include an assessment of employees' perceptions and attitudes regarding management. One aspect of such perceptions and attitudes is revealed in the relative volume of employee grievances and in the manner in which employees choose to deal with such matters.

[redacted] I have become concerned about the increasing number of grievance cases handled by my office and about the fact that too many employees appear to be bypassing normal grievance handling channels to bring their cases directly to the Inspector General. The Agency's grievance handling mechanism is outlined in HR [redacted] which defines a grievance as:

> "an employee's expressed feeling (oral or written) of dissatisfaction with any aspects of his working conditions and relationships which are outside his control." 25X1A

The procedure described in HR [redacted] by which employees may seek prompt and equitable consideration and disposition of their grievances includes:

- Recourse to the immediate supervisor or others within the normal chain of command in the employee's own component if the supervisor does not arrange a satisfactory resolution of the problem. Though not stated in the regulation, this normal chain of command includes individual grievance officers in each of the Directorates;

- Review of the problem by the Director of Personnel if a satisfactory adjustment is not reached in the employee's own component; and

- Appeal to the DCI through the Inspector General if the employee is still dissatisfied. The DCI's decision is final according to HR [redacted] 25X1A

25X1 [redacted] The Inspector General's function in the grievance handling process is described as follows in HR [redacted] which outlines my responsibilities: 25X1A

> Provide a forum wherein CIA personnel may, on a highly confidential basis, confide grievances or complaints that have not received satisfactory consideration through normal channels of command. The Inspection Staff is empowered to accept direct appeals from employees when appropriate.

In fulfilling this function, I act as the staff adviser to the Director and his Deputy. When formal decisions on grievance cases by the Director or his Deputy are required, my advice takes the form of recommendations

---

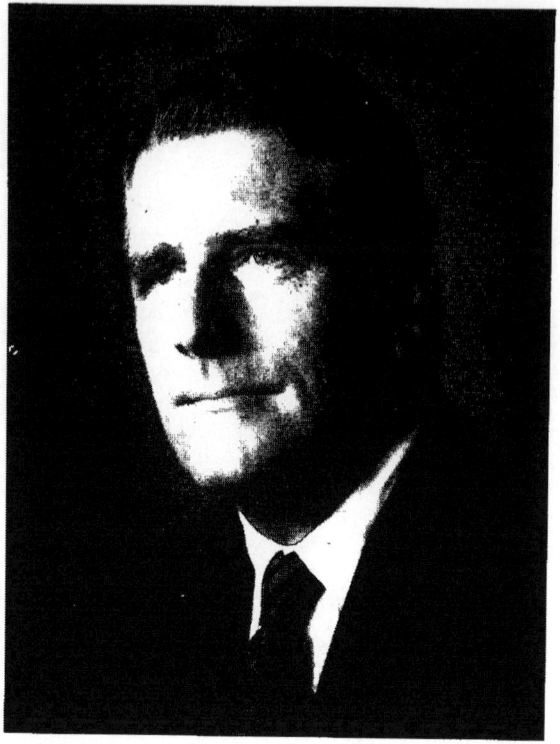

John H. Waller Inspector General

CANDID CAMERA: "60 Minutes"

On 24 July 1977 a vignette introduced CIA to the audience of CBS's "60 Minutes." In the July 1977 DDA Exchange the DCI commented:

> While the presence of camera crews in the Agency for more than a week was at times an inconvenience and involved some security problems which had to be resolved, I believe in the long run it was well worth the effort. A large audience across the country will see inside the CIA for the first time when that program is aired. Hopefully, they will learn for themselves that we are ordinary people, dedicated to serving our country well in an organization which fulfills a vital national need.

The candid shots, taken by an OL/P&PD photographer, show the CBS crew at work.

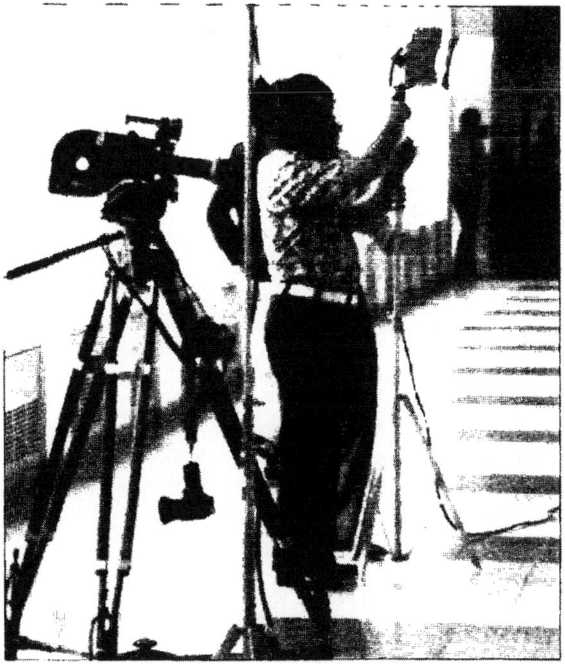

CBS camera crew sets up equipment

Form **1040** Department of the Treasury—Int
U.S. Individual Incor

For the year January 1–December 31, 1977, or other taxabl

e IRS label.
erwise, print
or type.

First name and initial (if joint return, give first

Present home address (Number and street, inclu

City, town or post office, State and ZIP code

Central Intelligence Agency
telephone directory

September 1977

FUNCTIONAL DIRECTORY

BLACK

Graphics Service:
Intel. Photos & Films (CLD/OCR) rm1E4822 Hq ....
OGCR Graphics ....
P&PD Graphics & Visual Aids rmGD79 Hq ....
Guard Posts—See Inside Back Cover
Handicapped & Disabled Veterans Program
inator rm836 Ames ....
ooms—See Dispensary

n1J45 ....
her Bldgs—Refer to Admin Officer
Merit Awards Board rm1D70 Hq ....
ization—See Insurance
ation—See Dispensary

TRANSMITTAL SLIP DATE

TO:

ROOM NO. BUILDING

REMARKS:

feature

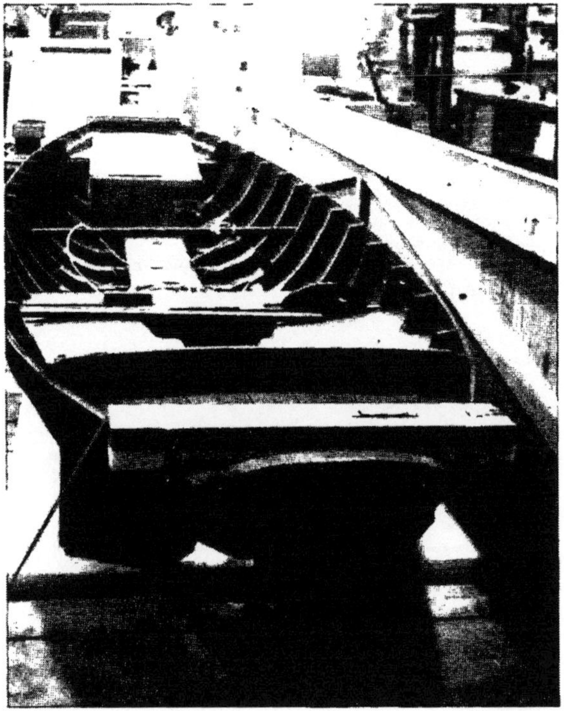

WRAP-IT-UP

[redacted] OL 25X1

[redacted] Packaging is defined as the use of containers and components plus decoration or labeling to protect, contain, and identify merchandise and facilitate use of products. 25X1

[redacted] Containers go back to the dawn of history. Any item to be stored or transported called for packaging. This led to the use of leaves, gourds, goatskins, turtle shells, earthenware pots and jars, reed baskets, and the like. Marks, signatures, symbols, and seals were produced by the Egyptians more than 4,000 years ago. 25X1

[redacted] The industrial revolution is generally credited with influencing the great advances in container invention and fabrication, resulting in the development of most of the 25X1

A Boat Being Packaged for Overseas Shipment

standard container forms used today. Included were the metal can, folding carton, collapsible tube (toothpaste), corrugated shipping case, and crown closure (crimped bottle cap). During the latter part of the 19th and the early part of the 20th centuries, the groundwork was laid for mechanized production of standard packages. During this same period, the development of Linotype, photoengraving, process-color printing, and additional graphic art processes completed the combination of container and effective decoration needed to make modern methods of packaging possible. An example of putting this new found technology to work originated with the Uneeda Biscuit Company. In 1899, the famous Uneeda Biscuit package was introduced. It is generally considered the event that signaled the end of the "cracker barrel era."

[redacted] Container and packing material production continued to experience phenomenal growth over the years. The reported value of packaging produced in 1939 was approximately $2 billion, in 1968 $17 billion, and in 1976 packaging production reached a record high of nearly $27 billion.

[redacted] Packaging in the Agency is also big business. The [redacted] maintains a large, well-equipped packaging section, staffed with experienced packers. During the last fiscal year, the [redacted] spent more than $325,000 on packing materials to pack some 35,000 line items. (A line item ranges from a single transistor to a complete SKYLINK unit.) Due to the sensitive and fragile nature of many items, it is necessary to package for a high degree of protection. Many methods and different materials are employed to meet the packaging requirements of the individual items and the method of transportation to be used.

[redacted] The [redacted] operates two fiberboard box making machines. With these two machines, custom made boxes can easily be fabricated to exact specifications. Many different sizes and styles of boxes are available along with several different types of fiberboard to satisfy almost any requirement.

Fiberboard boxes of predetermined sizes are stocked for day-to-day usage. The Box Shop has the capability to produce both plywood and wooden boxes in numerous styles and almost any size specified. Wooden boxes are used in surface and air shipments, packaging of large and/or heavy items and for special applications requiring multiple use containers.

[redacted] maintains a substantial inventory of many different types of packaging materials required in the packing and crating function. Custom molded polystyrene boxes are used for high volume items requiring a high degree of physical protection. The expanded polystyrene boxes are molded at a commercial manufacturing plant, using Agency-owned molds designed for specific Agency equipment.

[redacted] Over the years, our packaging personnel have developed a number of techniques to deal with specific packaging problems. When typewriter motors began breaking loose during shipment, a technician developed a stronger mount which IBM liked so well that they awarded him $1,000 for the idea. Medical serums and some film require refrigeration during transit. A specially designed ice holding, polystyrene container handles these quite well. Solid state circuit boards for electronics systems now have their transportation jolts cushioned by a special container.

[redacted] The packaging and transportation of items such as pesticides, paints, and photographic chemicals have become increasingly regulated in the past several years because of hazards involved in their transportation and storage. Spray cans, for example, may explode in the unpressurized hold of an airplane. Such materials must be packed, marked, and certified in compliance with strict Federal and commercial regulations to avoid serious penalties and fines. Several employees at [redacted] have been qualified by the Department of Defense to certify that hazardous cargo is packed in accordance with specific regulations to meet the method of transportation being used.

25X1

25X1

25X1

Next 2 Page(s) In Document Exempt

confidential

Directorate of Administration

confidential

confidential

october 1978

dda exchange

confidential

Men do not stumble over mountains, but over molehills.

Confucius

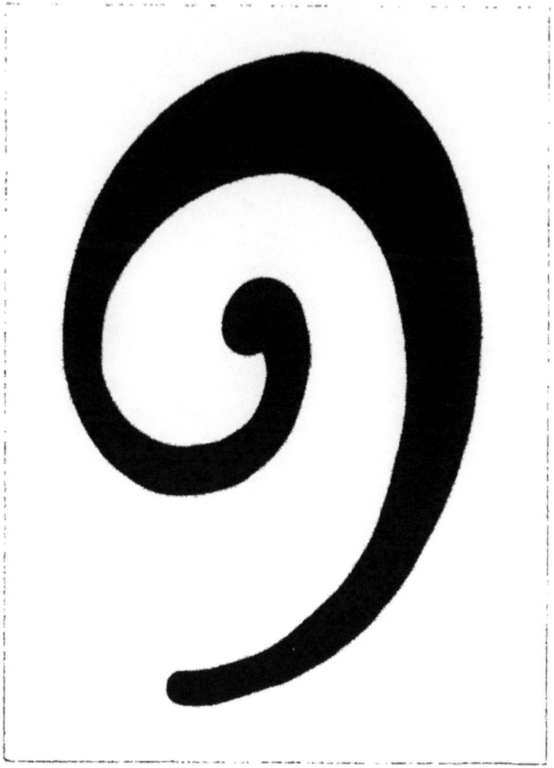

dda exchange

A quarterly publication for the exchange among DDA personnel of ideas, concepts, information, and techniques that are of common interest.

NATIONAL SECURITY INFORMATION

Unauthorized Disclosure Subject to Criminal Sanctions

Classified by 000288
Exempt from General Declassification Schedule
of E.O. 11652, exemption category:
§5B(1), (2), and (3)
Automatically declassified on:
date impossible to determine

25X1A

staff

SENIOR EDITORS

[redacted]

MA[redacted]

index

VOLUME 3, NO. 4

comment

IT IS TIME TO FIGHT BACK—Public Affairs at the CIA

The phone rings often in the Public Affairs Office:

— the WASHINGTON POST: "Did the CIA try to assassinate Prime Minister Manley of Jamaica?"

— Jack Anderson: "Was a CIA agent in Dallas named Morris Bishop a friend of Oswald's in 1963?"

— TIME: "Wants confirmation on wire story saying CIA is helping the West Germans build a missile test site in Zaire."

A few years back the answer to all three inquiries would have been easy enough to provide—"NO COMMENT."

The answers we did provide:

— "Absolute and utter nonsense;"

— "The name Morris Bishop has never been used as an alias or pseudonym—nor has anyone with that name ever been employed by the CIA;"

— "Ridiculous—there is no such activity underway."

Times have changed. The country has changed and so has public affairs at the CIA. It is time to fight back—to tell it like it is. We still use "no comment" when we have to. But as the DCI said in a recent speech, "Our needle isn't stuck in that groove anymore."

Why change now? The DCI believes that no government agency can operate in today's world without public understanding and support. Unfortunately, CIA lost much of its public support as a result of the various executive and congressional investigations, the series of anti-Agency books and articles, and the reams of paper released under the Freedom of Information Act. The CIA suffered enormous criticism—some warranted, much not. The blind confidence of the public

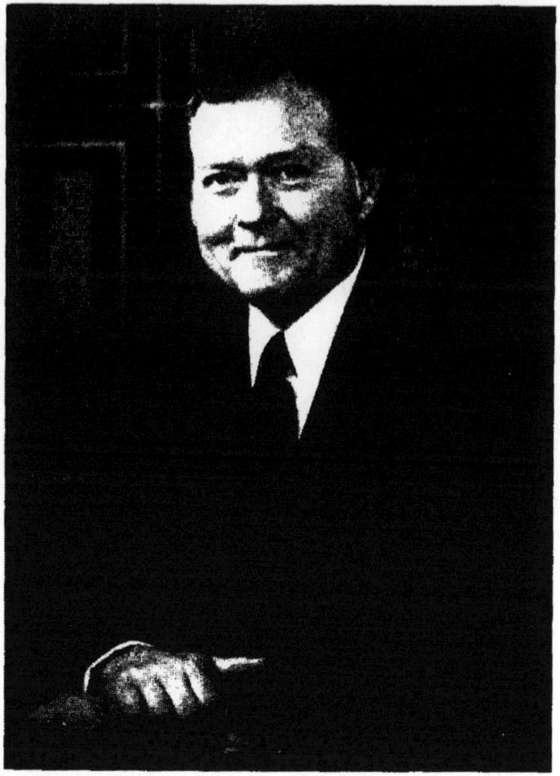

Herbert E. Hetu
Director of Public Affairs

about dda

25X1

Underway on a body of water of any size, where the safety of your boat and its crew is at stake, it's not "where you ought to be," or "where you think you are," but your knowledge of "where you are for sure" that counts.

Charles F. Chapman
from *Piloting, Seamanship and Small Boat Handling*

INDEX

FROM MOTHBALLS TO UTILITY

[redacted]

25X1A

Next 4 Page(s) In Document Exempt

SECURITY ESCORT PROGRAM

[redacted] III, OS

Since its inception in 1965, the Security Escort Program, an integral part of the Security Services Section, Headquarters Security Branch, has grown from a staff of 13 full- and part-time contract employees to its current level of 68 escorts.

The primary purpose of the program is to provide an escort service for the Headquarters complex and outlying Agency buildings to facilitate access of uncleared construction, installation, maintenance, and char personnel. Each day approximately 35-40 escort requirements are levied upon the Security Services Section by OL. The jobs requiring security escort service range from bricklaying to computer installations. They cover the Headquarters Building from its basement storage closets to the seventh floor roof. For each activity, Security Escorts are responsible for signing in and badging the work crews, escorting them, and signing them out at the end of the working day. Escorts work when the technical crews work and must be available 24 hours a day.

The Agency and OS attach a great deal of importance to the "watch and report" aspects of the program. This service provides essentially a first line of defense against penetration via the guise of a private contractor. Each Security Escort, shortly after entering on duty, is given comprehensive briefings designed to familiarize him with detection and reporting procedures for suspect packages and "bugging" devices. In a similar vein, each escort is cross-trained in basic safety and health emergency procedures. A third element of training is familiarization with OS, its procedures, and its regulations.

In addition to the basic escort activities, the program assists in providing security coverage for media events, public tours, and special support assignments. The program has provided security building access to:

- CBS television crews and personalities during filming of a "60-Minutes" segment on CIA;
- ABC for its "Good Morning America" sequence; and
- *Time, Newsweek,* and *National Geographic* magazines for their pictorial essays.

Late last year, during Project OUTREACH, Security Escorts assisted in processing tour groups during visits to the Agency.

What types of individuals make up the Security Escort corps? Most are young men and women who are still enrolled in local universities or are very recent graduates. The program allows them the opportunity to work for the Agency while still completing degree requirements. These young students are complemented by others who provide diversity of experience and backgrounds.

By substituting for staff personnel who would otherwise have to perform escort duty and by expediting the movements of uncleared personnel in Agency facilities, the Security Escorts provide a cost-effective, professional service.

(UNCLASSIFIED)

confidential

Directorate of Administration

confidential

january 1979

dda exchange

secret

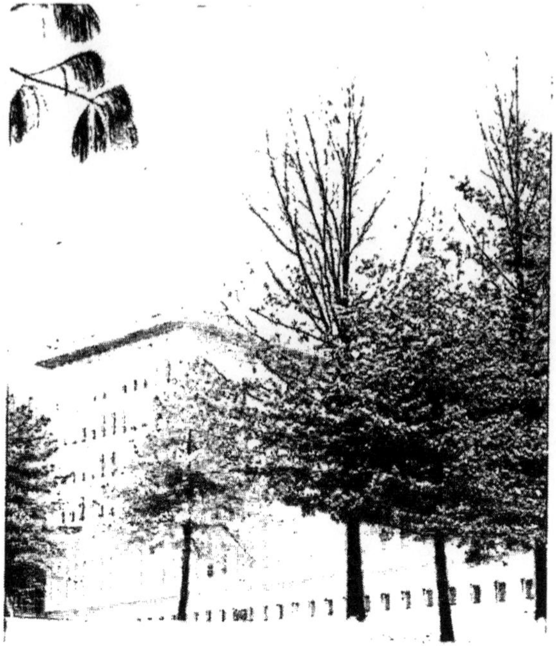

Tell me and I'll forget,
Show me and I may remember,
But involve me and I will understand.

OTR

dda exchange

A quarterly publication for the exchange among DDA personnel of ideas, concepts, information, and techniques that are of common interest.

NATIONAL SECURITY INFORMATION

WARNING NOTICE
Intelligence Sources and Methods Involved

Photographs in this issue carry the overall classification of the article in which they appear.

staff

index

VOLUME 4, NO. 1

comment

For those in the DDA who have had the opportunity to serve abroad, you can readily appreciate the close cooperation—in fact, the actual integration—that takes place in melding the functions of the DDO and the DDA into a single Agency mission abroad. That integration process is vital to the work of the DDO and indeed instrumental in assisting the DDO in accomplishing what it does.

The ease of the effort between operations and support stems from a history shared by both directorates, reaching back to the OSS during World War II. While there may have been various permutations in the wiring diagrams of each respective component, the end result was the same: effective support to our operational activities. As the mission of the Agency evolved from large-scale paramilitary and covert action programs to an emphasis on the traditional espionage, the job of support to our operations became more difficult. Dwindling positions overseas required that the DDA do its job with fewer personnel, yet the complexity of our operations increased, and the accountability became more stringent. No longer was it sufficient to accomplish the difficult, but to do so with complete regard for propriety, legality, and efficiency. As we moved from large support structures in our overseas stations to what is now referred to as "minimum manning," we called upon the DDA to insure that we continue to enjoy the best of support and also to take additional care that our stations' finances, logistical records, and personnel needs remain in good order. 25X1

The fact that the DDO wears a variety of covers in its overseas activities places an added burden upon the process of administering our personnel abroad. Whether that is done through an executive department's organization, through a nominal arrangement, or through a nonofficial cover entity, we have an insatiable desire for our needs to be satisfied with a standard throughout and take for granted the timely administration of a dozen or so different payrolls. The mission of the Agency has been paramount in the lifestyle of those who support our operations

John N. McMahon
Deputy Director for Operations

the directorate

MAJOR CHALLENGES IN 1979 [redacted]

In this, our first *DDA Exchange* issue of the new year, the Office Directors were asked to share with readers their answers to the question:

What is the major challenge that your office faces in 1979? [redacted]

COMMUNICATIONS [redacted] 25X1

[redacted] 25X1A

Accommodating changes in our operating environment is the major challenge to OC today. [redacted] 25X1

Overseas perks are disappearing while inflation and the shrinking dollar, along with crime and terrrorism abroad, are making overseas living less and less attractive to our personnel. Nevertheless, we must keep hundreds of highly motivated, conscientious, professional communicators working 25X1A throughout the world. [redacted] 25X1

[redacted]

Throughout these changing conditions, we must continue to operate an effective, efficient worldwide network accommodating ever increasing volumes of traffic while simultaneously facing decreases in fiscal and human resources. Although the challenges of 1979 may be somewhat unique to our organizational history, the men and women of OC have always met challenges with considerable flexibility and imagination. Next year will not be an exception.

DATA PROCESSING

Clifford D. May

In the 15 years that ODP has been in existence, it has grown into one of the most diversified and technically sophisticated computer facilities in the country. This sophistication has been brought about by ODP's efforts to bring computer support as close as possible to the end user and to simplify its use. The computer is no longer the sole domain of the computer professional but is now the day-to-day working tool of the budget and fiscal officer, the logistics officer, the personnel officer, the intelligence analyst, and the office secretary, to name a few. At their fingertips, we have placed the ability to perform such diverse tasks as economic modeling, word processing, text analysis, statistical computations, and graphic presentations.

To maintain, improve, and broaden this type of computer support to the Agency and the Intelligence Community, ODP must attract and retain a complement of highly skilled, competent, and imaginative specialists, far superior to those required in a more static and conventional computer installation. In light of the salary ranges, working environments, and fringe benefits available in the private sector to computer specialists of this caliber, the major challenge facing ODP in 1979 is the recruitment, compensation, and retention of personnel with sufficient skill to allow the Agency to continue to enjoy the breadth and depth of computer services to which it has become accustomed—and without which it can no longer function effectively.

FINANCE

Thomas B. Yale

"Doing more with less" has become a recurrent theme throughout the DDA and the Agency over the last several years, and OF is no exception.

A multitude of forces continues to converge on this one common point. Executive and Congressional interest in the execution of Federal agency programs in general and National foreign intelligence programs in particular have prompted demands for more financial and budget related data both internally and externally. Controls, checks and balances over the use of official funds are being continually fine tuned in response to internal management and external oversight requirements. New interpretations or reaffirmations of old attitudes, some of which have taken the form of a Privacy Act or a Freedom of Information Act, have generated new administrative requirements. 25X1

While meeting these challenges and concurrently striving to adapt "state of the art" technology to CIA financial and budgetary requirements and processes, OF also continues to play its traditional day-to-day roles of accountant, auditor, banker, and paymaster. All of this we have and must continue to do with limitations on our only resource—people. 25X1

Our challenge then, in 1979, is to find ways and means of maintaining the continuing integrity of Agency financial operations and meeting demands for more information on a timely basis while, at the same time, streamlining and improving procedures consistent with "state of the art" technology and otherwise improving the overall cost effectiveness of our operations. [redacted]

LOGISTICS [redacted]

James H. McDonald

The major challenge facing OL will be to conclude action started 3 years ago with GSA to lease approximately [redacted] square feet of space, design and configure to our requirement, and effect the moves required to meet increased demands for space in the Headquarters Building. [redacted]

Our needs for more space stem from a variety of requirements, primary of which is the conversion of Headquarters offices to special-use space for expanding computer-oriented programs (such as SAFE). Additionally, we are seeking to alleviate the extremely crowded conditions in Headquarters Building as well as accommodate new functions that must be located in Headquarters Building. As always, the key issue and most difficult decision to make is who (and which components) will be required to move out of Headquarters Building into the newly leased space. OL is charged with developing recommendations for EAG decision on this sensitive and controversial subject. [redacted]

MEDICAL SERVICES [redacted]

Charles A. Bohrer, M.D.

While I can see the value of identifying the challenge, which in essence would amount to predicting the future, I have become very humble and cautious about doing so for a variety of reasons. [redacted]

However, given continuation of past level of support for OMS mission and function by senior management, the major challenge has been and continues to be the recruitment and retention of qualified personnel. That challenge could, in short order, be turned to a different challenge if this office should be reduced in strength. The major challenge then would be deciding what function would be eliminated. Reduction in strength by salami-slicing is no longer possible. Any reduction would require discontinuance of a service or a function. [redacted]

PERSONNEL [redacted]

F. W. M. Janney

The major challenges facing OP in 1979 are:

- Development and institution of modifications to the Agency's personnel management system in accord with the DCI's decisions relative to policy changes and emphasis. [redacted]
- Collaterally institute efforts to improve visibility and employee understanding of the primary features of the promotion, career development, and comparative evaluation systems. [redacted]
- Monitor and evaluate personnel management as implemented through delegations of authority and responsibility to the Heads of Career Services and their Subgroups. [redacted]

SECURITY [redacted]

Robert W. Gambino

The greatest challenge facing OS in 1979 relates, as might be expected, to a recent and awesome case of espionage involving a former Agency employee. It also ties in to a significant number of other cases over the past 18 months where classified information has been improperly removed from Agency buildings or revealed to unauthorized persons. [redacted]

The crux of the challenge lies in strengthening security discipline and increasing employee motivation toward the goals of the security program. Key to all this is involvement; involvement by managers, by supervisors, and by all Agency employees. With such involvement (read "caring"), there are no security threats we cannot meet successfully. To promote such motivation, through security awareness programs, is our greatest challenge as we enter the new year.

TRAINING (U)

Harry E. Fitzwater

OTR faces a double challenge. The first is to meet a number of new requirements in such fields as management training, analyst training, and operations training. The other task is to improve the effectiveness of all OTR training programs by making sure that individuals who receive training participate to the fullest and that they demonstrate, as part of their training, accountability for the subject matter which is covered.

THE PHOTOGRAPHERS [redacted]

[redacted]OL

From time to time, articles have been published in *DDA Exchange* describing some of the unique activities performed by DDA careerists. We have read about the communicators, the occupational health nurses, the couriers. This article describes the photographers—those assigned to the Photography Branch of the Printing and Photography Division. And how better to "write" about their activities than in pictures? [redacted]

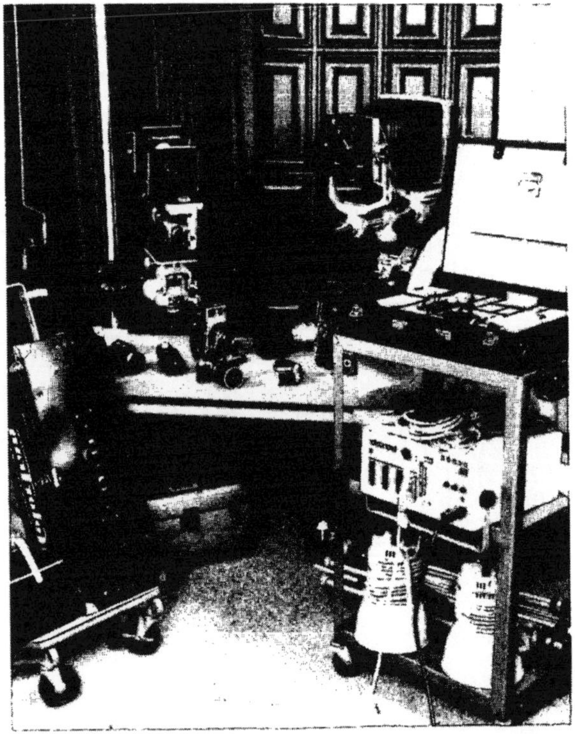

Part of the "photo team" and a variety of equipment that is frequently used to record the photographic requests. [redacted]

P&PD photographers busy "doing their thing." Note that the photographer must be close to the action and involved for a successful picture. The President's rapid movement makes focus difficult. Therefore, camera and light are pre-set and many quick grab shots are taken.

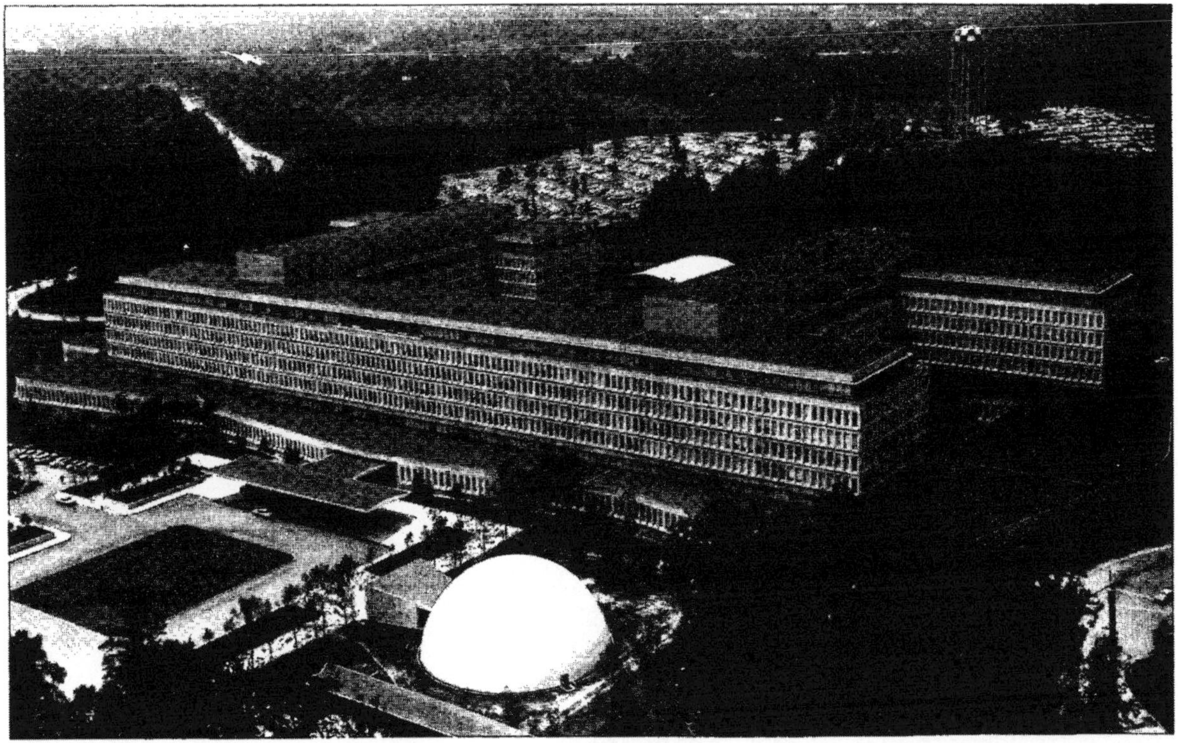

Aerial photo taken from helicopter. Doors are removed from aircraft before leaving ground to facilitate ease of camera movement. This also makes the job much more thrilling for the photographer! □

USING PSYCHOLOGICAL TESTS FOR PERSONNEL SELECTION: COMPUTER PROGRAMMING [redacted]

[redacted] Ph.D., OMS

The selection of personnel best suited to an office's working environment has typically depended upon interview data, previous job histories, and references. Selection can often be significantly improved through the use of tests which successfully identify persons who possess the skills, abilities, attitudes, habits, or personality traits required by the particular job. However, EEO guidelines have been the cause of great concern to managers and employers who are accustomed to making employment decisions based upon results from tests or other selection procedures. According to the *Federal Register* (Vol. 42, No. 251, 30 December 1977):

> The use of any selection procedure which has an adverse impact on the hiring, promotion or other employment or membership opportunities of members of any racial, ethnic or sex group will be considered to be discriminatory and inconsistent with these guidelines, unless the procedure has been validated in accordance with these guidelines . . [redacted]

Therefore, the problem arises in which one must choose a selection procedure which differentiates between persons who are able to perform the job in question and those who are not and which satisfies the requirements of using validated personnel selection procedures as set forth in the EEO guidelines. The solution to this difficult issue is to employ a valid test. [redacted]

What is a Valid Test?

Formal test validation is a necessary part of any effective personnel program which uses tests in order to facilitate the selection of qualified employees. The validity of a paper and pencil test is usually defined in terms of the relationship between scores obtained on the test and ratings obtained on some observable criterion, such as performance on the job. When a person's score on the test is high and the individual's job performance rating is also high, a positive correlation exists between the two measures. If the magnitude of the correlation is sufficient, we call the test a "valid" indicator of the job performance criterion. A properly validated test can be used as a selection tool which can predict an applicant's potential for success in the job—before he is hired. Validation studies of this type are instrumental in responding to two concerns frequently voiced by management:

- Are we rejecting high quality applicants?
- Are we expending valuable time and resources by processing many applicants who will probably never develop the skills necessary to perform efficiently on the job?

Test Validation Applied to Computer Programming

The Psychological Services Staff (PSS) of the OMS regularly conducts studies to validate existing paper and pencil tests. PSS has recently completed a validation study for ODP using information from the commercially available Wolfe Aptitude Assessment Battery for Programming (AABP), the Agency's own Professional Test Battery (PTB), and recent ODP supervisory job performance ratings. The study, conducted in close coordination with ODP, was designed to determine how well job performance in computer programming can be predicted from data obtained on psychological tests.

It was found that both the AABP and portions of the PTB are highly valid predictors of overall job performance in computer programming. Statistical analyses were performed relating scores on the AABP and PTB to ratings of job performance on each of four dimensions: programming performance

(PP), programming aptitude (PA), management/supervisory potential (MS), and systems analysis aptitude (SA). The results clearly substantiate the predictive value of the AABP and PTB on all four dimensions of job performance and especially for the dimensions PP, PA, and SA. This, of course, underscores the value of both the AABP and the PTB as predictors of subsequent programming performance and as a yardstick for estimating pure programming aptitude and systems analysis potential. [redacted]

PTB as an Applicant Prescreening Device

In addition to being a valid predictor of computer programming job performance, the PTB has been demonstrated to be immensely useful in predicting scores on the AABP test. The excellent predictability of performance on the AABP is, in addition to being interesting, of substantial practical significance. Agency applicants are tested using the PTB in [redacted] across the country. Field testing with the PTB can therefore serve a useful prescreening function. This could result in the saving of large sums of money currently being invested in the administration of the comparatively expensive AABP to many questionable candidates for professional data processing careers in the Agency. Results of scores on PTB tests could also provide a basis for deciding whether or not to bring the applicant to the Headquarters area for interviews and/or further testing. [redacted]

Who can benefit?

Any component involved with ADP functions, such as NPIC, OWI, ODP, OD&E, and IMS can apply the results of this validation study in selecting personnel with aptitude for computer programming. [redacted]

The PSS is prepared to make predictions of suitability for placement in jobs requiring general programming ability or other specific ADP skills, using PTB. While such predictions will probably never be error-free, they are better (by a very considerable margin) than guessing, and, when used together with other available information such as interview data, additional tests, references, or previous job histories, these validated predictions can play a tremendously important role in improving the employee selection process.

[redacted]

Copies of the full 83-page report describing the study in detail are available. Questions and/or requests for copies of the report may be directed to the author of this article, Room 706, Chamber of Commerce Building.

[redacted]

aids

INDEX

CPR—TO SAVE A LIFE

An OC Employee

Imagine how you might feel if a colleague or family member suffered a heart attack, and you had to live with the knowledge that you had been unable to help because you did not know how to administer cardio-pulmonary resuscitation (CPR). Perhaps it would have been too late anyway, but would you ever really be certain? An OC employee recently found himself in a situation where immediate CPR was required. With presence of mind, and a knowledge of CPR, this man saved a life.

The employee and his wife were stationed at a remote overseas location where the health care available was minimal. Following is a sequence of events leading up to the necessity for the employee to administer CPR to his wife.

The wife's first symptoms were nausea and severe pain, at first isolated in her left armpit

Next 3 Page(s) In Document Exempt

Directorate of Administration

secret

july 1979

dda exchange

> The rung of a ladder was never meant to rest upon, but only to hold a man's foot long enough to enable him to put the other somewhat higher.
>
> Thomas Huxley

dda exchange

A quarterly publication for the exchange among DDA personnel of ideas, concepts, information, and techniques that are of common interest.

NATIONAL SECURITY INFORMATION

WARNING NOTICE
Intelligence Sources and Methods Involved

Photographs in this issue carry the overall classification of the article in which they appear

staff

SENIOR EDITORS

index

VOLUME 4, No. 3

the directorate

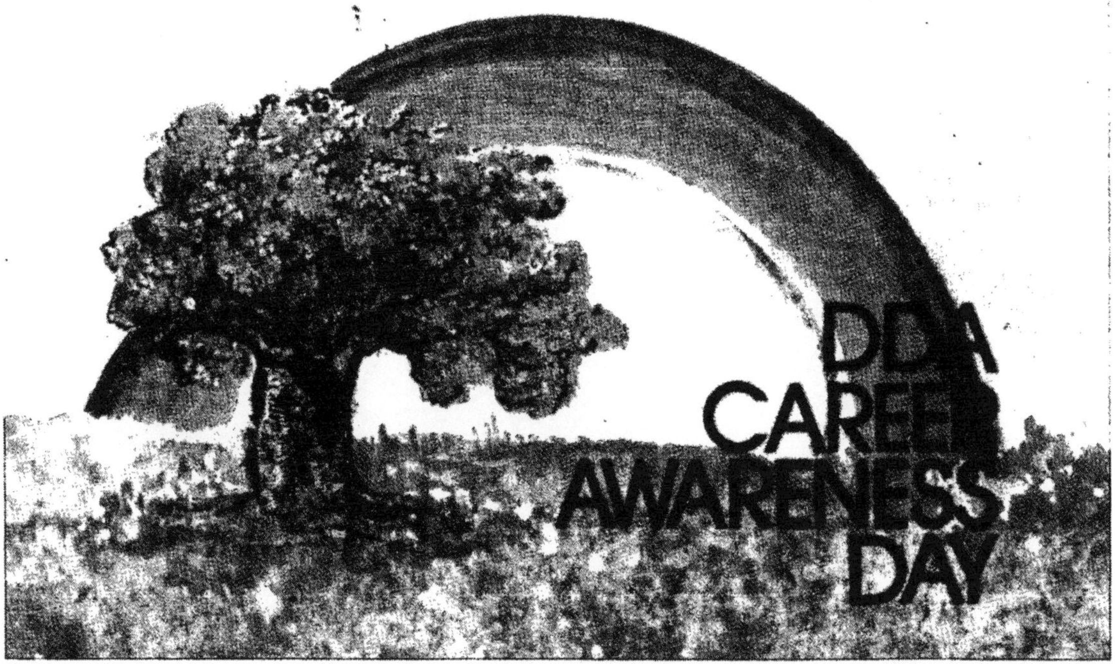

DDA CAREER AWARENESS DAY [redacted]

[redacted] OTR

Sponsored by the DDA Federal Women's Working Group, 6 June was designated as DDA Career Awareness Day. Preceding the formal program in the Headquarters Auditorium, at which both the DDCI and the DDA spoke, the participants were provided a look at the career opportunities in the DDA. Exhibits were displayed by all offices in the Directorate, and questions were answered by representatives who are Career Management Officers and Personnel Officers, and by other personnel from the offices. [redacted]

[redacted]

[redacted] Chairman of the DDA Federal Women's Working Group, opens the program. (U)

Next 15 Page(s) In Document Exempt

At first the Commission devoted all of its time to solving the problems of the public areas. Foremost was the fact that the entire interior of the building was painted a grey color usually reserved for the sides of battleships. The Commission sought assistance from a professional interior design firm. The jointly recommended plan included white walls and the standard color doors, which became the basis for the interior design plan as it exists today. The plan has subsequently been expanded to include color accent walls in conference areas and in the stairwells. [redacted]

As the walls changed from grey to white, a need arose for wall hangings. Working closely with the Logistics Services Division of OL, the Commission bought and mounted a variety of wall decorations including: London Transport Posters, Art Exhibition Posters, Potomac River Photographs, art reproductions, and color fabrics. [redacted]

Once the problem of the public areas had been addressed, the Commission turned its attention to the offices and the employees. A network of Environmental Committees was organized to enable the Commission to reach more people. Wall hangings were more widely distributed. A part-time design consultant was hired by OL to work with the Commission and to provide advice and guidance wherever it was needed. [redacted]

Today the Commission continues to seek ways to improve public and private areas. It meets monthly to address an agenda of items which ranges from the state of grounds around the Headquarters Building to an improved system of signage. The Commission is always looking for suggestions and new ideas and may be contacted through its Chairman [redacted], 4E32 HQS. [redacted]

Tunnel—supergraphic painting selected from 40 entries in Tunnel Design Competition . . . painting by volunteer employees. [redacted]

Main Corridor—paintings loaned from the Vincent Melzac Collection.

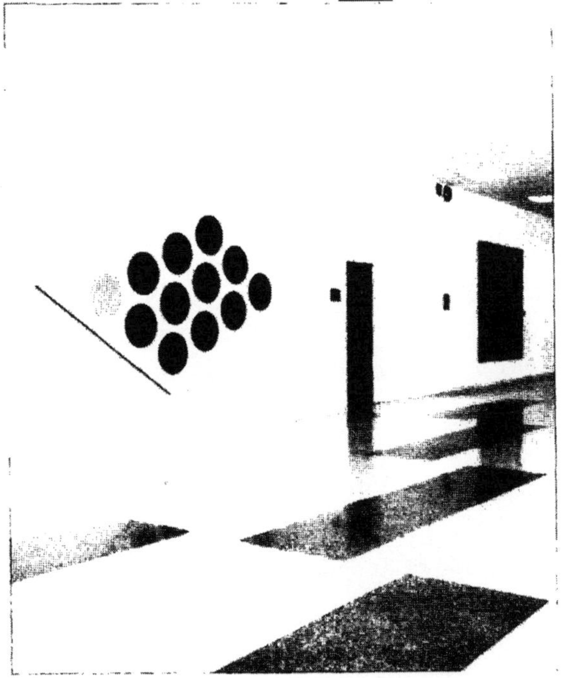

NUCLEAR WEAPONS ORIENTATION ADVANCED COURSE [redacted]

[redacted] OTR

The Interservice Nuclear Weapons School, under the aegis of the Air Training Command, and located at Kirtland Air Force Base, New Mexico, conducts six courses on a regular basis, with the Nuclear Weapons Orientation Advanced (NWOA) leading the pack in requirements. For over 15 years, the CIA has been a regular customer for this training, with an Air Force allocation to the Agency, via OTR, of approximately 80 spaces each fiscal year. NWOA is a five-day course, carries no tuition charge, and using offices fund approximately $450 in travel and per diem per student. [redacted]

In 1976, OTR's Training Support Division asked its contacts at the Air Training Command and the Interservice Nuclear Weapons School if the School's Mobile Training Team would consider conducting a running "on site" of the regular NWOA for Agency personnel. The result was the first such course, conducted in the Headquarters Auditorium in December 1976, with 102 Agency students and five from the Defense Intelligence Agency (DIA). [redacted]

Again in January 1978, the Team conducted another such course for OTR, this time in the C of C Building, with 41 Agency and five DIA students in attendance. Learning in January 1979 that the Mobile Training Team would be conducting courses for the National Security Agency and the Federal Preparedness Agency, OTR again requested the Team to include CIA on its itinerary. The result was an abbreviated two-day NWOA conducted in C of C 26-27 April 1979. Fifty-four Agency students attended, with representatives from NFAC, DDS&T, DDA, and DDO, one from NITC, and five from DIA. Coverage included:

- Nuclear Weapons Community, Principles and Materials;
- Arming, Fuzing and Firing;
- Stockpiled Weapons and History of U.S. Stockpile;

New Developments and Future Nuclear Weapons Concepts;
Blast and Thermal Effects;
Initial and Residual Nuclear Radiation;
Worldwide Fallout;
Nuclear Weapons Phenomena;
Nuclear Weapons Testing;
Command and Control of Nuclear Weapons;
Tactical Nuclear Weapons Employment; and
Antisubmarine Warfare Concepts. [redacted]

Total savings to the Agency in travel and per diem costs by arrangement of these on-site courses have been approximated at $60,000. [redacted]

At the opening of the recent course, OTR was pleased to present the CIA Seal to the Interservice Mobile Training Team. [redacted]

[redacted]

25X1A

Next 2 Page(s) In Document Exempt

secret

Directorate of Administration

secret

DDA/MAS OFFICIAL RECORD COPY

confidential

october 1979

dda exchange

confidential

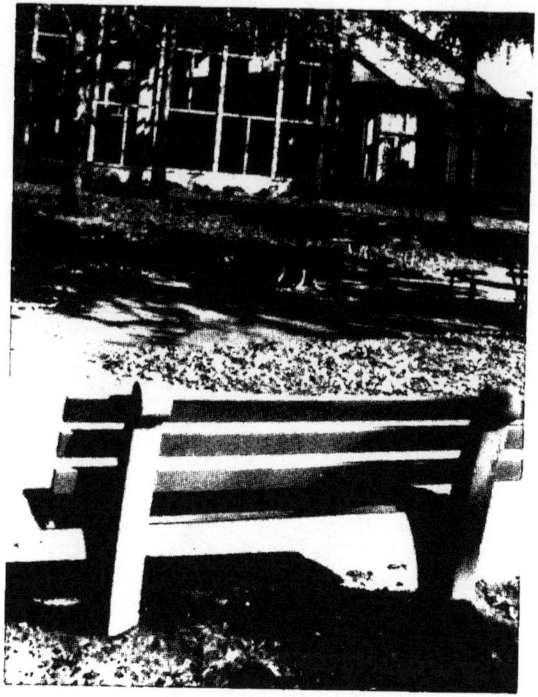

You'll get no laurel crown for outrunning a burro.

Martial

dda exchange

A quarterly publication for the exchange among DDA personnel of ideas, concepts, information, and techniques that are of common interest.

staff

index

VOLUME 4, No. 4

comment

As Director, Equal Employment Opportunity, one of my biggest problems is misunderstanding. Like other managers, I produce reports, implement programs, gather information, coordinate, provide guidance and leadership, and cope with resource cuts. However, much of my time, energy, and effort is consumed by the necessity of dealing with the emotional reactions to false perceptions of "EEO" and "Affirmative Action." The justification for all our plans, programs, and efforts under these titles is logic, morality, and law. Everything required of us is directed toward satisfaction of CIA's obligations as a federal agency. In brief, CIA is not being asked to "do something stupid."

Because much of the history of our society reflects systematic and continuing discrimination against minorities and women, laws have been provided to prevent future persecution and to help compensate for past damage. CIA, like other federal and state agencies and private institutions, is trying to comply with the spirit and letter of those laws. We cannot single-handedly heal the effects of a country's social ills. However, we are determined to guarantee equitable consideration to all applicants, potential applicants, and employees. We are determined to carry out affirmative action plans and programs to do something where historically we had done little. (The statistics of our early years would seem to indicate that minority hiring and female professional development "quotas" were zero. They were met consistently.)

25X1

Open hostility and the epithets—*broad, wop, nigger, spic, kike,* and all the rest—have, for the most part, fallen out of sight. However, the disappearance of overt manifestations of discrimination causes us to focus on the "covert" and on the subtleties of disparate effect—deliberate or unintentional. We see vacancy notices that demand unrelated degrees or other requirements when what is often needed for selection is a specific ability demonstrated by performance, knowledge, skill, experiences and relevant formal education—in short, the dem-

Omega J. C. Ware, Jr.
Director, Equal Employment Opportunity

perception

THE FEMALE SECURITY INVESTIGATOR— THERE'S NOT MUCH DIFFERENCE [redacted]

[redacted] This meant that daily I was dealing on a one-to-one basis with the non-CIA public as a government agent. Previously, the image of the government agent conducting investigations was primarily male. Therefore, was I treated differently by the public due to the fact that I was female? [redacted]

My first reaction to this question was no, there were no differences between myself and my male coworkers. However, taking a more objective and truthful viewpoint, I do recall distinct reactions and attitudes that might be attributable to my being female. [redacted]

Basically, the dominating response that comes to mind is surprise. The public in all areas, from academia to private industry, initially responded to my female presence and job-related questioning with astonishment. After this initial reaction, if the individual being interviewed were female, I would be frequently asked as to how I gained such employment. These individuals seemed genuinely eager to learn of such job opportunities and pleased to discover that women were branching out to new career areas. [redacted]

25X1

25X1

Continuing with the positive public reaction, I personally sensed that being a woman helped to establish a freer and more open conversation between myself and the individual being interviewed. My public image was more on the lines of a friendly confidante rather than the stereotyped image of the stern government agent. Furthermore, my presence posed no physical threat to individuals opening their front doors and inviting me into their homes. [redacted]

25X1

Occasionally, the initial response of astonishment of dealing with a female investigator

25X1

was followed by what I perceived as a negative reaction. My credentials were at times questioned and closely scrutinized. Female clericals and secretaries, as well as professional interviewees, particularly in security related fields, exhibited resentment toward me. This might well be attributed to a feeling of personal envy on their part or their own
25X1 perception of me as a threat toward their job security. Additionally, interviewees would at times interject sexual overtones into the conversation or become uneasy when I was required to ask direct and intimate questions related to personal behavior. These situations were always overcome by changes in my approach in that I would portray myself in a more aggressive and professional light. Although investigations are sometimes viewed as an infringement of the right to privacy, this type of negative reaction expressed toward me seemed to be no different from that occasionally experienced by
25X1 my male coworkers.

In conclusion, subtle differences in public response to a woman investigator do occur. These differences are basically positive and beneficial in nature and, in my opinion, do not make a significant impact either way on the finished product. Women should be treated and judged as individuals rather than being looked upon as a group bearing a minority label. They are definitely an asset and greatly needed resource in the security field.

25X1

Next 4 Page(s) In Document Exempt

25X1A
25X1

DDA FEDERAL WOMEN'S PROGRAM WORKING GROUP ELECTS NEW OFFICERS [redacted]

[redacted] OTR

The DDA Federal Women's Program Working Group works closely with the Federal Women's Program Board to ensure equal opportunity for women, identify problems and issues, promote activities to increase the awareness of DDA personnel concerning Agency and Directorate goals and programs for women, make recommendations as appropriate, and annually report on progress and accomplishments. The current officers were elected on 26 July 1979. [redacted]

The Group welcomes your comments and suggestions. [redacted]

25X1A

[redacted]

confidential

Directorate of Administration

confidential

secret

february 1980

dda exchange

secret

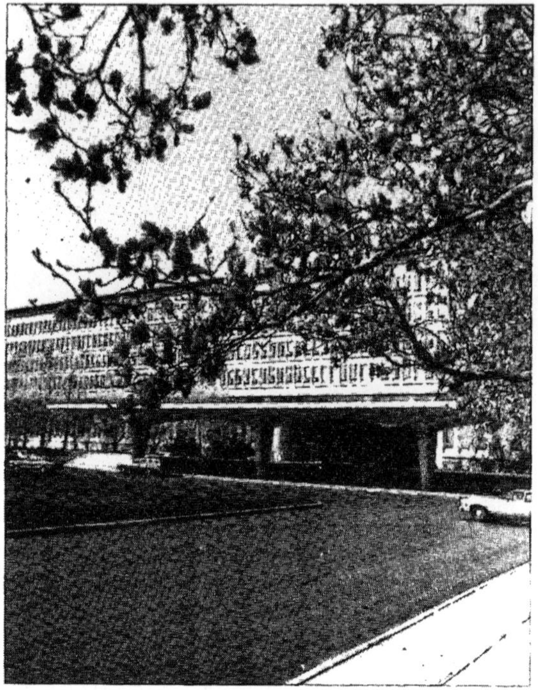

What is now proved was once
only imagined.

William Blake

dda exchange

A quarterly publication for the exchange among DDA personnel of ideas, concepts, information, and techniques that are of common interest.

NATIONAL SECURITY INFORMATION

ORIGINAL CL BY 219807
☐ DECL ☒ REVW ON 20 Jan 80
EXT BYND 6 YEARS BY same
REASON 3d3

WARNING NOTICE
Intelligence Sources and Methods Involved

staff

[redacted]

OTR
ODP
OP
OS
ISS-DDA
OMS
OL
OC
OF

MS-DDA

MS-DDA

index

[redacted]

VOLUME 5, NO. 1

comment

In August 1979, Mr. Bruce C. Clarke, Jr. became the Director of the National Foreign Assessment Center. This issue's COMMENT is based on a talk given by Mr. Clarke to NFAC employees in November. (U)

I would like to discuss the context in which I see NFAC operating and the role of the National Foreign Assessment Center. (U)

The Context

The context of NFAC's work obviously is that of supporting the Director in his role as Chief Intelligence Adviser to the President and to the government. The degree to which we are effective in doing that measures how well we can feel about what we are doing. I think so far the record is good. I hope we can improve it. (U)

The Agency's mission, and NFAC's in particular, is to be an important source of intelligence analysis to the United States Government. What all components of the government share is a hunger for knowledge, for facts, for information, for understanding, for new ideas, new perceptions. Most of the time they hope that the intelligence judgments of NFAC and their own judgments will coincide, and they are much more receptive to NFAC's view if they do. But they are prepared to put up with them if they do not. (U)

In this regard, the main point I would make is that NFAC does not and cannot serve any single constituency. Rather, there is a diverse set of officials with diverse interests. There are the policymakers, high and low, the would-be policymakers, and the staffs of policymakers. There are also all those folks laboring in the vineyard—whether it is DIA or INR, the Departments of Energy or Commerce—who are our colleagues in intelligence analysis. Given the range of people for whom our work is vital, it is difficult to contemplate NFAC production or an NFAC response solely in terms of a single user or single individual. (U)

There is another important constituency, one which has emerged in important ways

Bruce C. Clarke, Jr.
Director
National Foreign Assessment Center

perception

NOTES FROM A SATISFIED USER (U)

[redacted] ISS-DDA

Funny, whenever I read that title, I feel as if I'm hooked on something. I guess in reality that I am hooked—on VM. Don't know what VM stands for—stay tuned. Not long ago, I didn't know what VM stood for either. Much less, I really didn't care. (U)

I returned from an overseas tour in 1976 to find OF in the midst of a jungle of new acronyms, GIMS, FRSORN, FRS1, GAS . . . where had I been? Now next to most adding machines sat a computer terminal. What scary things! And these gray monsters with typewriter keyboards and television screens had taken over my job! There is no fighting, no turning back; this is the new system. But, it took years to learn the debits are by the window, or is it the credits are by the window, and now—you say that only one entry is needed! Don't expect me to change overnight. (U)

The change was not overnight, nor was it easy. I was so fixed in my ways (I liked the old system!). That is, until I was convinced that the new system is better. I don't think anyone ever said, "Hats off to the GAS team" or "How did we operate without GAS?" but I'm saying it now! It's hard to remember what it was like before, but now I'm dedicated to the new system. (U)

My thanks to those hard-working innovators is not only for changing the system, but for changing me. My attitudes are completely different now from the time I returned and reported to ODP in March 1977 as a Finance Officer. Thank goodness I accepted the enemy and found a reconciliation. I am continually amazed at what can be done by those fantastic machines which once were such a threat. (U)

Soon after reporting to ODP, I found out, not only did the General Accounting System exist, but I could use the computer for my own job. This was unbelievable, but true. The capabilities of VM (Virtual Machine) are infinite. (U)

Because of my introduction to computers, I began to ask how could computers help. It all started with two safe drawers full of files and ended with a drawer one-fourth full and a RAMIS file that handles all the contract records for ODP/Budget & Finance. In less time than I can check one hard file, the Rapid Access Management Information System (RAMIS) can sort through the contracts, select certain ones, add them, subtract them, locate invoices, and provide an impressive printout with any column headings that I desire. (U)

The update of the files is much the same as with the hard copy files, but now it can all be done without leaving the terminal. And after the information is loaded into the system, it can be handled more effectively and efficiently than one person is physically capable of doing. (U)

Through the development of my files, I learned a lot about computers and a lot about people. ODP'ers are a great help, and they are probably the ones who get the most excited about a satisfied user and a program that works. Rather than developing the programs themselves, they enjoy helping you understand the workings of your own program. I don't owe ODP a thing except everything that I have learned from them. As I begin a new job, I will never forget how they helped me. Especially at times when the book was at an end (I couldn't find an answer), I was at an end (I couldn't solve a problem), or the world was at an end (I had erased my files). They put the computer in my hands and taught me how to use it. I no longer fear the system! (U)

Now the whole scene has changed. When I began working on my program in the front office of ODP, there were two users in that office. I was able to use the terminal whenever I wanted. When I departed that office in October 1979, there was a line for terminal use. There are now ten users in place of those original two. Everyone is beginning to realize that computers can make life easier. The best place to start to realize the importance of computers is in the courses offered by ODP. These courses are the best help

COMING: SPRING AT HEADQUARTERS (U)

These pictures, taken by staff photographers of the Printing and Photography Division, OL, can remind us of one kind of beauty in store for Headquarters personnel once winter leaves our midst. (U)

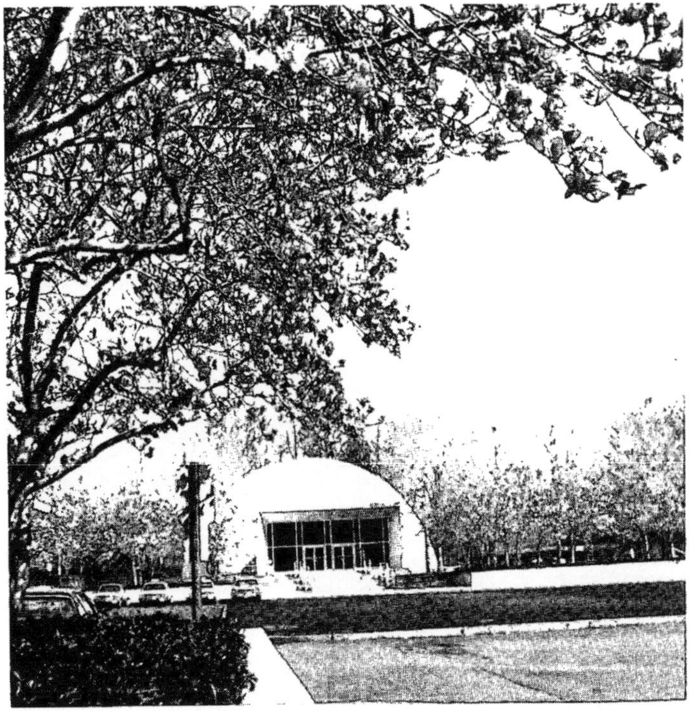

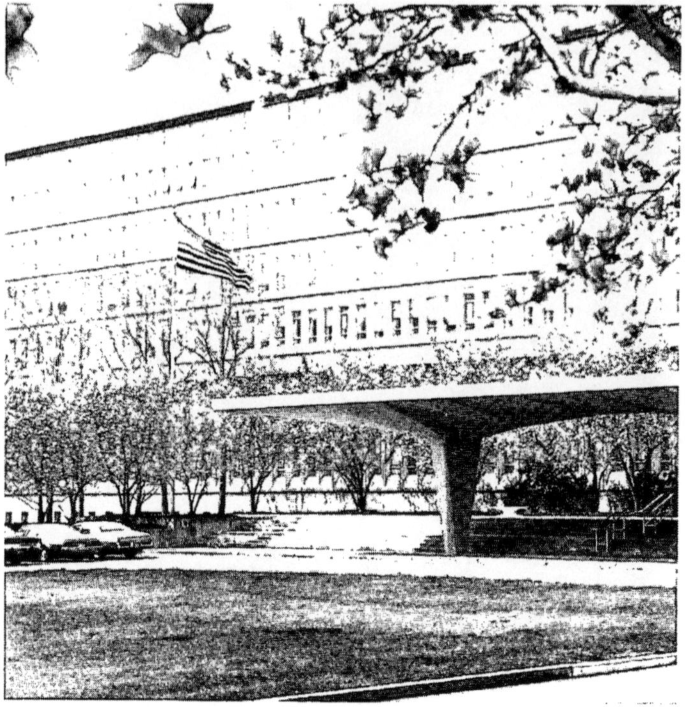

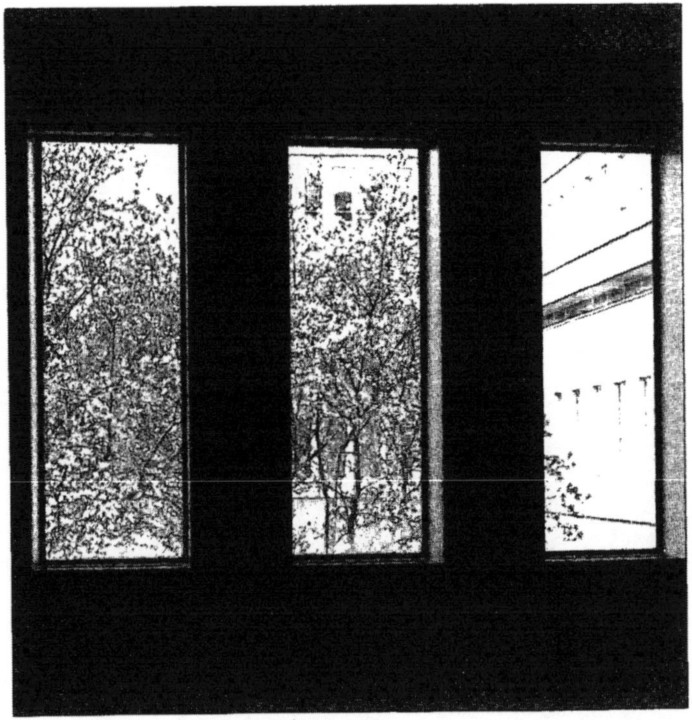

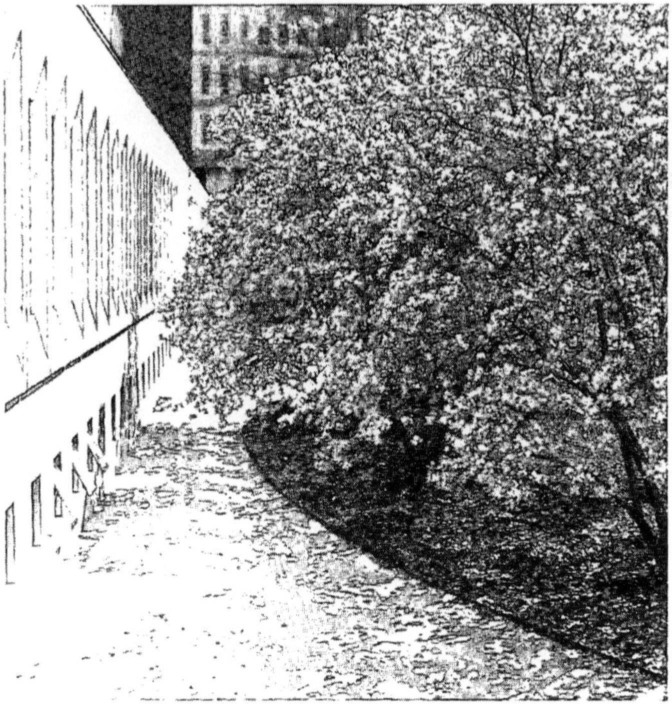

INFORMATION SERVICES STAFF

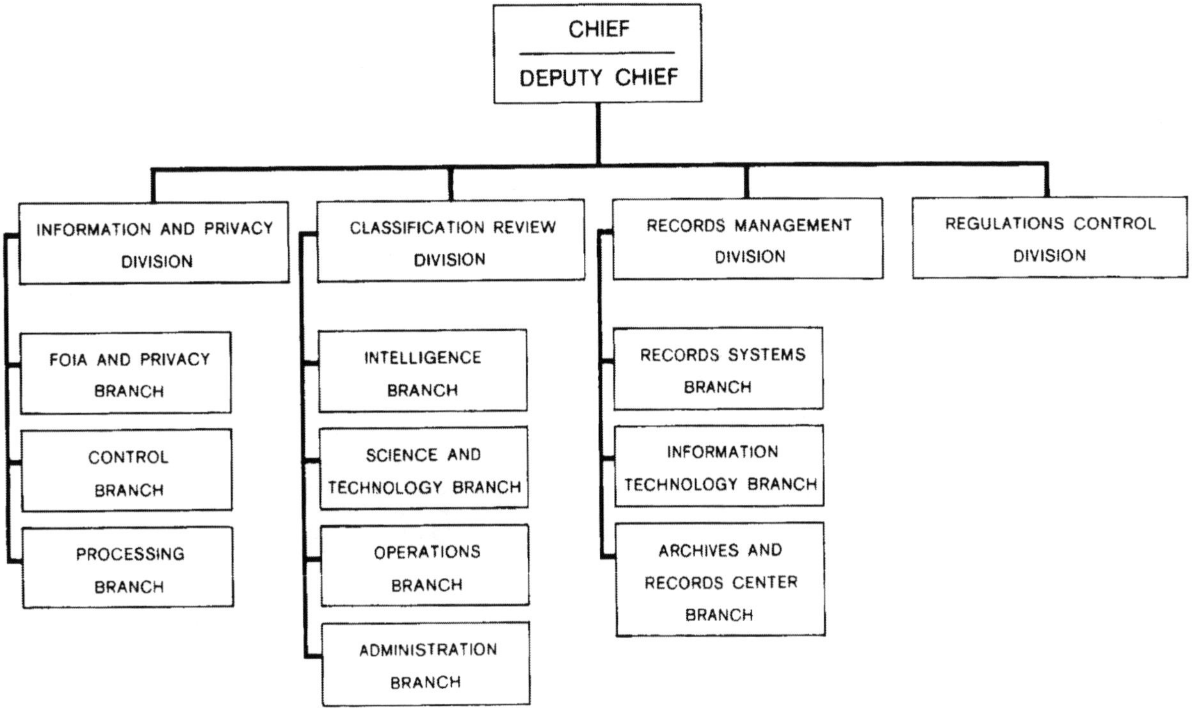

note

PAPER SIZE CONVERSION (U)

[redacted]L (C)

In December 1978, the Congressional Joint Committee on Printing authorized 8½x11 inch as the government stationery standard size effective 1 January 1980. That action directly affects all office stationery stocks, including letterhead, bond second sheets, manifold tissue sets, and carbon paper. The present stocks of these items are 8x10½ inches. The Committee approved the use of both stationery sizes until the 8-inch stocks were depleted with the proviso that: "all reasonable, orderly, and economical means are used to deplete existing Federal stocks of 8 inch stationery and related paper." (U)

The National Archives and Records Service has developed the conversion procedures that all federal agencies must follow to ensure a reasonable, orderly, and economic transition. Some examples of these are:

- Use all existing stocks of 8x10½-inch stationery including letterhead, plain bond, manifold carbon tissue sets, and carbon paper.
- In preparing correspondence, intermix stationery sizes if that is the only method that will deplete 8x10½ inch stock.
- Ensure that the size of self-addressed return envelopes can accommodate the size documents to be returned.
- Consider using 8½x11-inch paper for new or revised forms that are commonly interfiled with correspondence. However, use existing stocks of 8x10½-inch forms before converting.
- When copying an entire document containing both 8x10½- and 8½x11-inch paper, use 8½x11-inch copy paper. (U)

All office machines currently in use in the Agency can accept either 8x10½- or 8½x11-inch paper or can be modified to do so quickly and simply by any service technician. (U)

Appropriate action has been taken by OL to begin replacing Agency stocks of 8x10½-inch paper with the 8½x11-inch size. The Printing and Photography Division/OL, with the concurrence of Information Services Staff, has also begun printing Agency forms on the new 8½x11 paper. (U)

Directorate of Administration

DDA/MS OFFICIAL RECORD COPY
DO NOT REMOVE FROM 7C18 HQS

secret

may 1980

dda exchange

secret

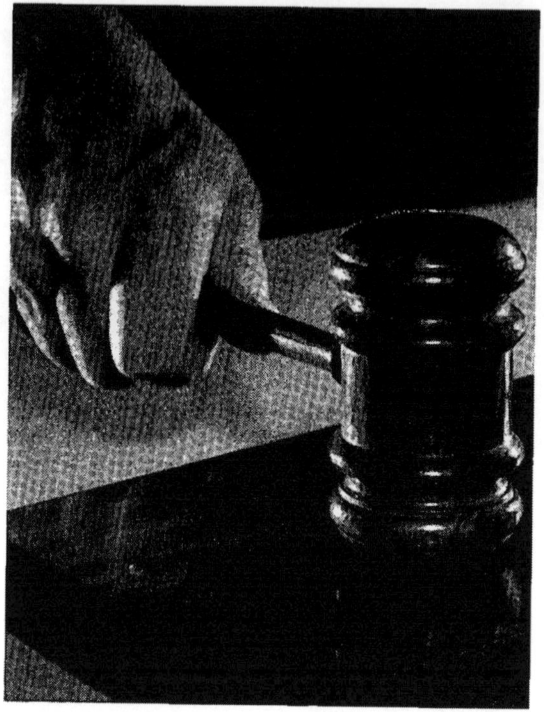

Laws should be like clothes. They should be made to fit the people they are meant to serve.

Clarence Darrow

dda exchange

A quarterly publication for the exchange among DDA personnel of ideas, concepts, information, and techniques that are of common interest.

NATIONAL SECURITY INFORMATION

ORIGINAL CL BY	219807
REVW ON	7 May 80
EXT BYND 6 YRS BY	same
REASON	3d3

WARNING NOTICE
Intelligence Sources and Methods Involved

staff

[redacted]

OTR
ODP
OPPPM
OS
ISS-DDA
OMS
OL
OC
OF

MS-DDA

MS-DDA

[redacted]
MS-DDA

index

[redacted]

VOLUME 5, NO. 2

comment

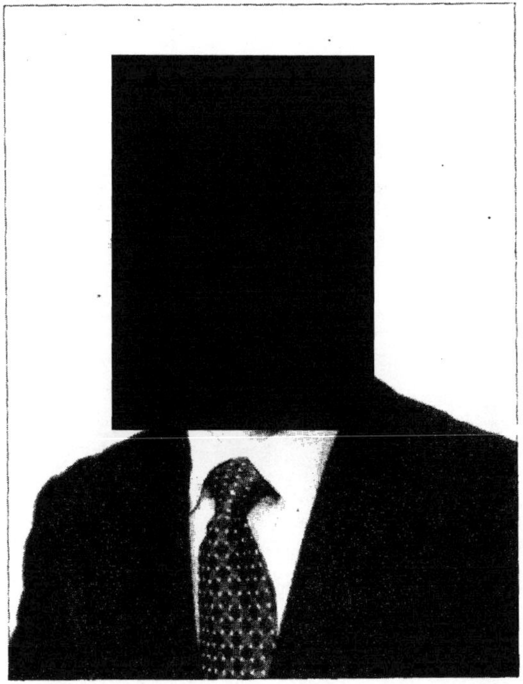

It is a pleasure to have the opportunity to tell you about the CIA's legislative program for this session of Congress. This is indeed an exciting and busy time for all of us in the Office of Legislative Counsel (OLC). One can almost daily find one or more of our legislative initiatives the subject of major news coverage. These initiatives represent programs or issues which will shape or significantly affect our Agency. The DCI and DDCI have spent much of their time and effort over the past year supporting these initiatives as part of their commitment to ensure that our country has a strong, effective, and responsive Intelligence Community operating within policy and legal guidelines. (U)

OLC

Before we discuss our promising legislative opportunities, I would like to describe

---

Frederick P. Hitz
Legislative Counsel

feature

THE LANGUAGE INCENTIVE PROGRAM (U)

[redacted] OTR

On 1 October 1979, the Agency embarked on a new effort that is expected to reverse the continuing loss of foreign language capabilities among Agency employees. The completely revised Language Incentive Program (LIP) has several features that make it attractive for Agency employees. (U)

One primary feature of the program is that each Agency component must identify positions that require a specific language capability. These identifications have been referred to as the Unit Language Requirements (ULRs). Following identification of these positions, the new program authorizes payments to individuals who are assigned to the positions and possess the requisite language skills. During the first five months of the program, more than 500 Agency employees have been declared eligible and are receiving a Language Use Award of an additional $50 in each biweekly paycheck. The payment provides compensation for their use of a foreign language in the position they occupy. (C)

Other features of the program scheduled to become effective in FY-81 are the Language Achievement and Language Maintenance Awards. Language Achievement and Maintenance Awards will be paid to nominated individuals who upgrade or maintain their skills in designated incentive languages. Schedules for achievement and maintenance award payments and information on eligibility are contained in [redacted] dated 6 September 1979. (U)

It is still too soon to tell whether the LIP can reverse the steady decline of language competence in the Agency. A meaningful review of its impact, as compared with prior years, will be completed at the end of FY-80. The Agency suffered a net loss of 16 percent of its minimum professional proficiency level or higher speakers between 1974 and 1979. There are indications that this persistent problem is being reversed with adoption of the new program. The following are some of the positive signs: Part-time language training, both in terms of numbers of employees and languages taught, has increased; proficiency testing has increased over 60 percent; overseas oral testing requirements have increased; and the Language School has had to develop taped tests to be sent to employees overseas and returned to Headquarters for scoring. These factors indicate renewed Agency personnel interest and activity in the use, achievement, and maintenance of foreign languages. (C)

The Agency has been most responsive to the recommendations of the President's Commission on Foreign Language and International Studies. The Agency's reemphasis of the importance of developing foreign language ability by its creation of an active program to increase the quantity and quality of language skills appears to mark a turning point in addressing the Agency's foreign language problem. (U)

25X1A

definition

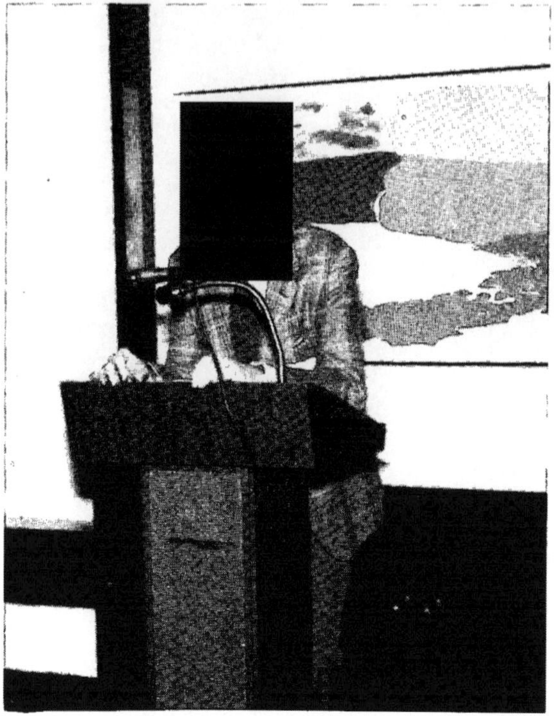

WHAT'S AN SSP? (U)

[redacted] CMO-DDA

In April 1978, the DDCI directed the Head of each Career Service in the Agency to establish a senior secretarial panel for the career management, development, competitive evaluation, ranking, promotion, and assignment of secretarial personnel in grades GS-08 and above within the career service. In compliance with the DDCI memorandum, the Administration Directorate established such a panel effective 15 May 1978. The DDA Career Management Officer, [redacted]

[redacted] Chairman, DDA Senior Secretarial Panel (U)

TECHNICAL LIBRARY (U)

[redacted] ODP

Do you need a basic computer programming manual, in-house documentation on how to write a cable using a terminal, or a copy of an ancient ODP *Tech Note?* Norma may have the material you need; visit GA3918 or call [redacted] the Technical Library of the Customer Services Staff, ODP and ask for her. (U)

The Technical Library stocks over 400 different IBM manuals, 60 manuals written in-house such as SCRIPTW and SEDIT, and documentation from approximately 40 vendors on computer software packages. It also contains over 300 reference textbooks on computer-related subjects available on a loan basis. The Tech Library makes this unique service available to anyone in the Agency who is dealing with computers, from the beginner to the expert. The Librarian tries to keep a step ahead of the user in the fast-moving data processing field, keeping in stock the "most wanted" manuals. Vendors routinely supply documents free of charge with the initial purchase of software or hardware; however, subsequent documents updating the software or hardware are likely to be very costly. (For example, the supplemental newsletters for Release 6 of the three basic VM manuals cost $11.50.) Copies of in-house documentation are made available through the duplication and binding services of the Printing and Photography Division, OL. Requests for other materials, such as textbooks, are accepted by the Librarian, and purchases are made through normal Agency acquisition procedures. (U)

The Tech Librarian distributes the ODP *Tech Notes,* which announce changes in the computing system, new software package documentation, or revisions of manuals which may affect the user. She keeps a distribution list of over 600 individuals for automatic receipt of the *Tech Notes.* You may call to be placed on this distribution list. (U).

The Technical Library cooperates closely with, but does not duplicate the services of, the main CIA Library and other Agency libraries. The Technical Librarian maintains liaison with the ODP Training Staff and knowledgeable systems engineers and analysts who recommend and review texts for incorporation in the library and notify the Librarian of updates or revisions of documentation. The Librarian always welcomes suggestions from you for new textbooks or documents which may be helpful to the general computer user. (U)

There are some limitations on service from the Technical Library which should be mentioned. Cost of some documentation is, of course, one limitation. Among others are the occasional lack of lead time in ordering manuals and the slowness of vendors in shipping manuals. Although a listing of

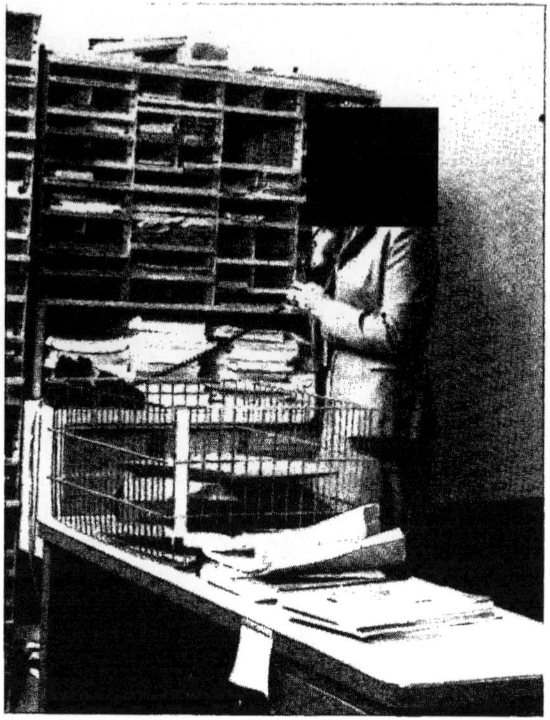

Technical Librarian [redacted] receiving phone request (U)

subscriptions of periodicals received in ODP is kept on file, the Library can house only a limited number of periodicals, such as the Auerbach Reports and IDC reports. One of the future goals is to improve this situation and eventually keep computer periodicals. Some government regulations are also on file such as Federal Information Processing Standards (FIPS PUBS). (U)

At last count, there were almost 2,900 users on the VM system alone; the size of this user group makes it impossible to mail to individuals everything they might like to have. However, the Technical Library is open from 0800 to 1400 daily, and if you visit room GA3918 between those hours, you may be able to immediately pick up or order the documentation. Alternatively, a user may call [redacted] to order documents which then may be picked up at the user's convenience. (U)

The Technical Library in Customer Services believes its function is to give the best possible service to anyone using computers and that nothing is more important to those users than obtaining the latest documentation available. If it is available somewhere, we will find it for you. Nothing pleases the Librarian more than to hear a customer say, "This is just what I needed" or "I didn't know this existed" or "This is the best collection of computer references around." The ultimate plan is to build a database of every manual available by number, subject, and title so that a terminal user could look at the list, choose what he or she needs, and have it mailed by an Automatic Mailing System. However, since this is in the planning stage at present, we will continue to try to help our customers as much as we can through the present system. (U)

Storage facilities for available technical publications (U)

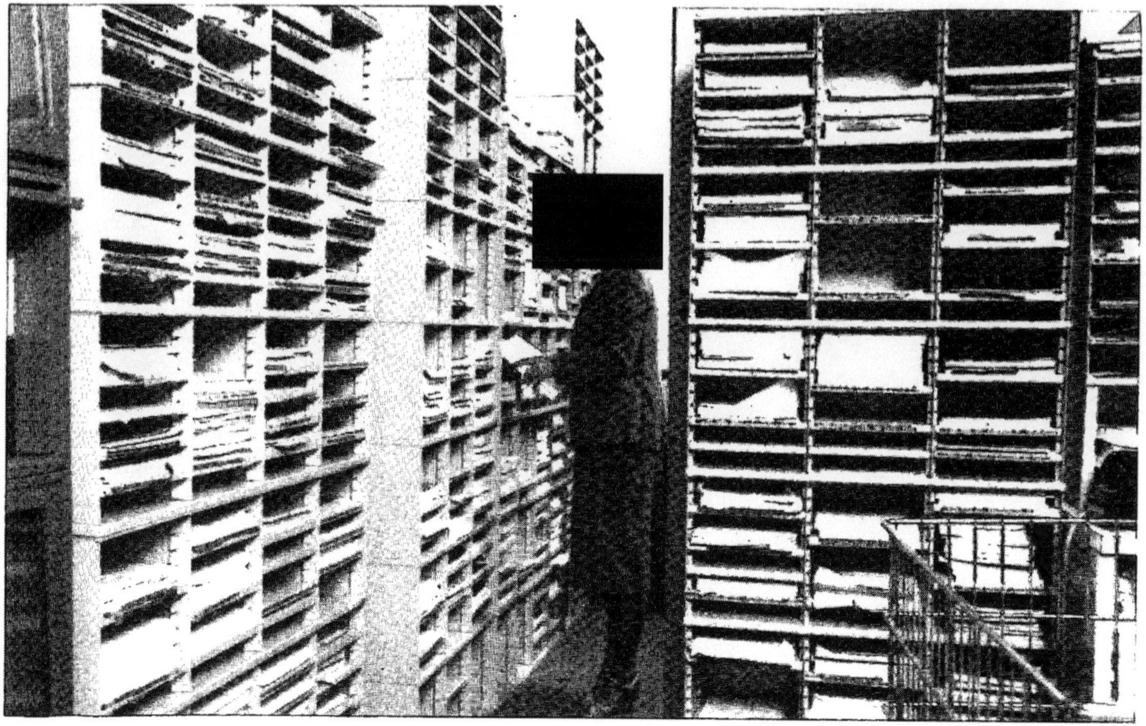

secret

Directorate of Administration

secret

august 1980

dda exchange

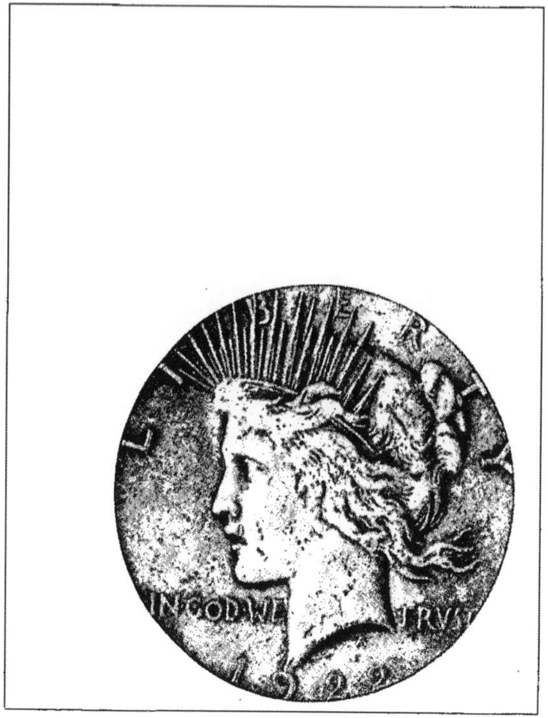

Never ask of money spent
Where the spender thinks it went
Nobody was ever meant
To remember or invent
What he did with every cent.

Robert Frost
The Hardship of Accounting

dda exchange

A quarterly publication for the exchange among DDA personnel of ideas, concepts, information, and techniques that are of common interest.

NATIONAL SECURITY INFORMATION

ORIGINAL CL BY	219807
☐ DECL ☒ REVW ON	30 Jul 2000
EXT BYND 6 YRS BY	219807
REASON	3d (3)

WARNING NOTICE
Intelligence Sources and Methods Involved

Photographs in this issue carry the overall classification of the article in which they appear

staff

SENIOR EDITORS

[redacted]

OTR
ODP
OS
ISS-DDA
OMS
OL
OC
OF

MS-DDA

MS-DDA

[redacted]CIATE

MS-DDA

[redacted]

index

VOLUME 5, NO. 3

comment

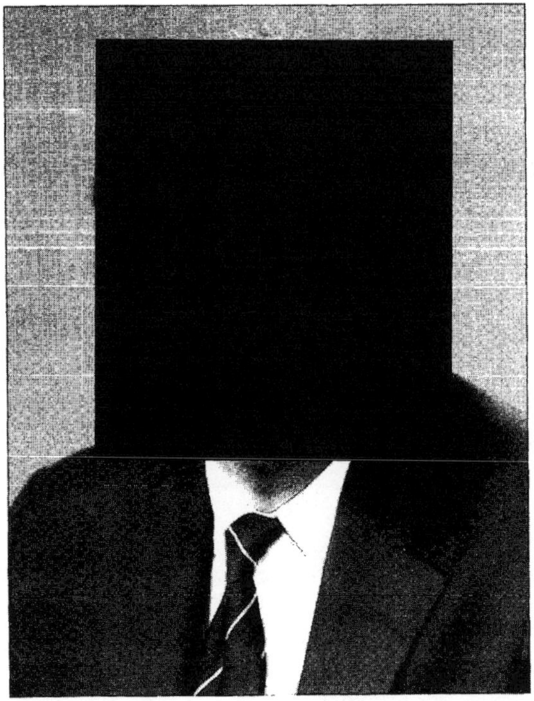

I'd like to use the next few pages to discuss the status of the CIA budget—the resources we all need to do our jobs. (U)

Our budget for this year (Fiscal Year 1980) has been increased; it is now considerably more appropriate to our needs than it was when the year began last October 1st. Our budget for next year, which is now midway on its path through Congress, should provide for an expanded CIA effort in 1981. The Executive Committee has approved our 1982 budget and sent it to the Director, where it will receive an Intelligence Community-wide review. 1982 holds out solid promise for substantial, needed growth. (S)

Those of you involved in the development of the 1982 program are to be congratulated for your professionalism and ingenuity. (U)

Maurice Lipton
Comptroller

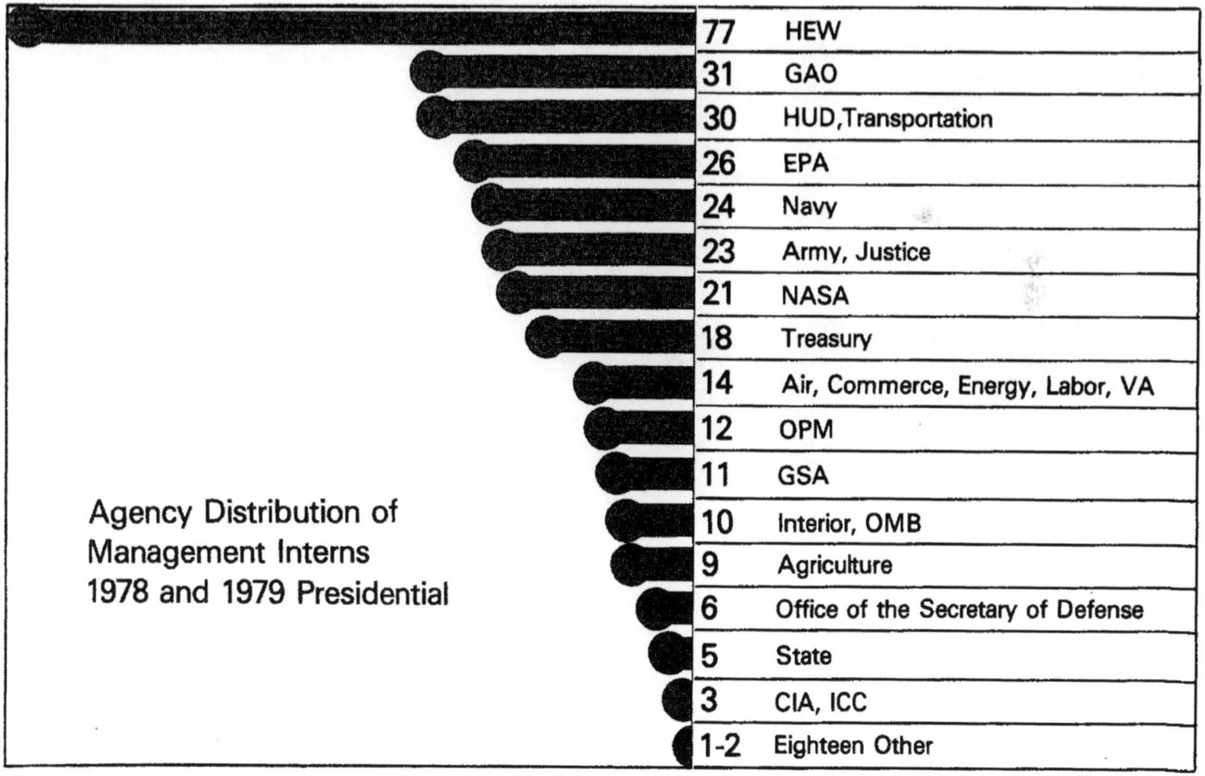
77 HEW
31 GAO
30 HUD,Transportation
26 EPA
24 Navy
23 Army, Justice
21 NASA
18 Treasury
14 Air, Commerce, Energy, Labor, VA
12 OPM
11 GSA
10 Interior, OMB
9 Agriculture
6 Office of the Secretary of Defense
5 State
3 CIA, ICC
1-2 Eighteen Other
Agency Distribution of
Management Interns
1978 and 1979 Presidential

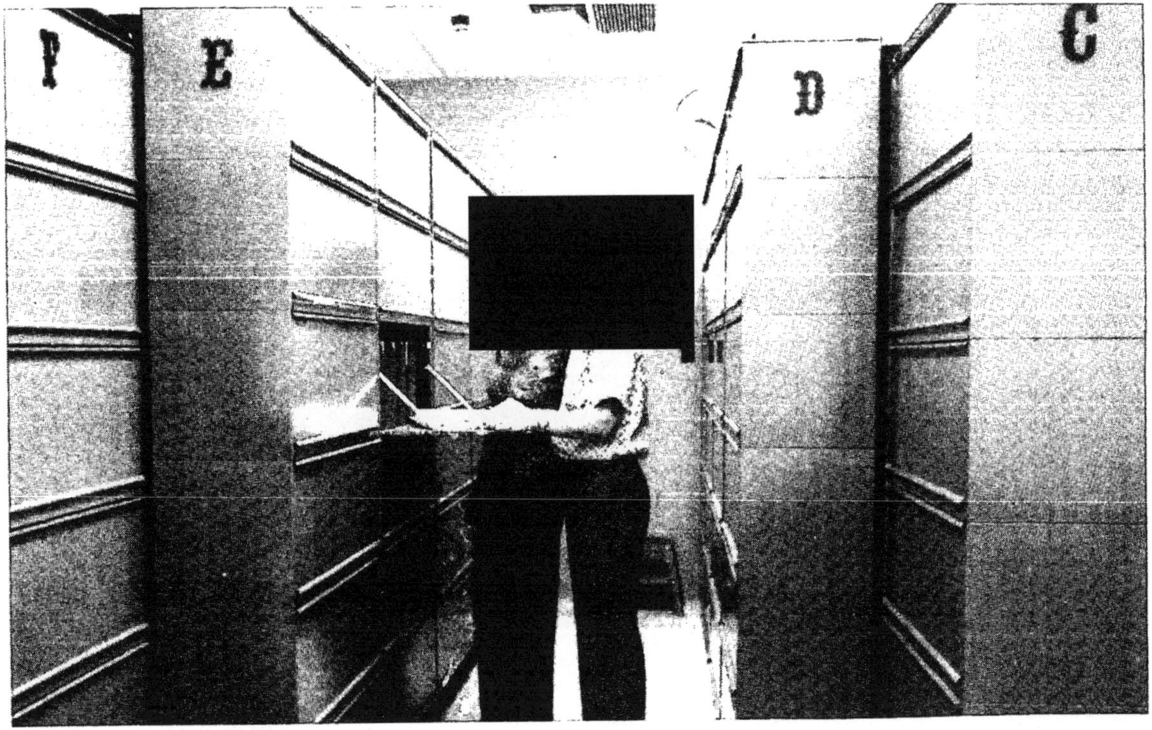
F
E
D
C

note

Within the next several issues, you will notice some changes in *Exchange*. We recently received approval to try some new ideas. Among them are:

— *Theme issues.* If you have any theme ideas, we'll take them. We tried a small version of the theme this time by having several articles, pictures, and quotations on MONEY.

— *Anonymous articles.* Send them to your office senior editor. Names are listed at the front of *Exchange.*

— *First person articles.* Has anything interesting happened in your job lately? It might be a candidate for an article. Not to let the rest of you off the hook—if something interesting hasn't happened, "business as usual," you still might have an article.

— *Current Events.* Offices will contribute a small paragraph about some new development. Give your ideas to our editors.

— *Authors from other directorates.* If you have a suggestion or if there is a particular non-DDA function which you would like to hear about, let us know. We have some plans to request articles from NFAC, DDS&T, and DDO, but we could always use more ideas.

— *Short articles.* A common misconception is that articles for *Exchange* have to be lengthy. If three or four sentences adequately say what you would like to say, we'll take it.

Final word—there is now quite a growing number of authors who have been published in *Exchange*. Why aren't you one of them?

"Being an editor is a hard job, but a fascinating one. There's nothing so hard as minding your own business, and an editor never has to do that."

Finley Peter Dunne

secret

Directorate of Administration

secret

dda in the 1990's

october 1980

dda exchange

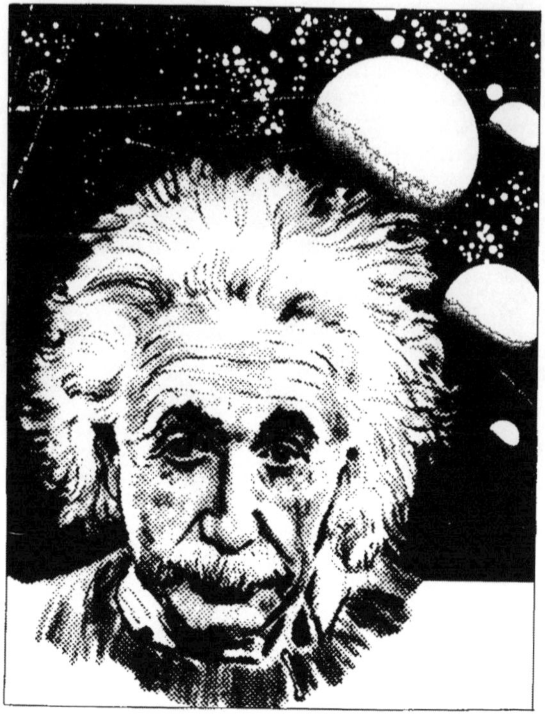

I hold that man is in the right who is most closely in league with the future.

Henrik Ibsen

help!

This is our first try at a theme issue, which we plan to publish about once every year. We would very much like your opinion on the Exchange, the theme idea in general, and the presentation of the "DDA in the 1990s" theme in this issue in particular. (U)

A questionnaire is included as the last page of the magazine. We would appreciate your taking a few moments to complete it. You may reproduce the form, or if you need additional copies, please contact the DDA Management Staff, 7D18 Headquarters, ex- [redacted]

dda exchange

A quarterly publication for the exchange among DDA personnel of ideas, concepts, information, and techniques that are of common interest.

NATIONAL SECURITY INFORMATION

ORIGINAL CL BY 219807
☐ DECL ☒ REVW ON 31 Oct 2000
EXT BYND 6 YRS BY 219807
REASON 3d (3)

WARNING NOTICE
Intelligence Sources and Methods Involved

Photographs in this issue carry the overall classification of the article in which they appear

staff

SENIOR EDITORS

[redacted]

ODP
OTE
OS
OIS
OMS
OL
OC
OF

MS-DDA

MS-DDA

OCIATE

MS-DDA

[redacted]

index

VOLUME 5, NO. 4

comment

[redacted] was the DDS&T representative to the Information Handling Task Force. His comment on Information Handling in the 1990s follows.

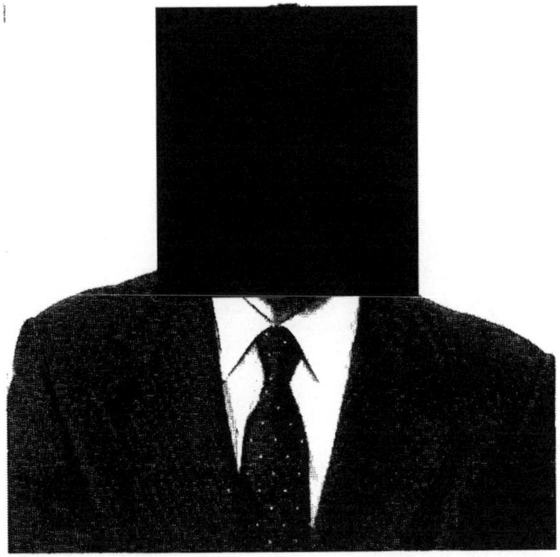

Advances in electronics, communications, and computer technology are truly breathtaking. Had automobile technology improved at the same rate, a Rolls Royce would cost $2.50 and get 200,000 miles to the gallon. We are in the midst of an information revolution, which, like the industrial revolution before it, will change the way we do our jobs, the jobs we do, and the organizational context in which we do them. Wistfully, this is one revolution where our Agency will not be in the van. Our needs pale beside the information needs of industry, our resources are Lilliputian beside the dollars to be spent for home computers, video disks, and electronic games. Having thus lost our ability to

---

[redacted]
Chief, Processing Analysis Technology Group, ORD

steer computer technology, we must be more alert to where it is taking us, as individuals and as an organization. (U)

Electronic "chips," soldiers in the information revolution, double in capacity roughly every two years, and resulting reductions in price, weight, and power consumption of memories and logic elements will make possible many new applications and improvements in present applications. Sensor and communications systems will increasingly output digital information, and the rates of data will increase dramatically. Computers will transform this data glut into useful information. Increased data processing at the sensor location will reduce the complexity of the problem at the central processor. (U)

Silicon Logic and Memory is the workhorse of the large mainframe computers used by the Agency, whose requirements in this area differ not at all from other government and private users of such equipment—i.e., millions of instructions per second (MIPS), storage disks, etc. at lower cost. By the 1990s, general purpose performance will range from 30 to 100 MIPS. Memory sizes will be two to eight times as large as those of today's largest computers; cost will drop and power consumption will be a few kilowatts. (U)

Micro- and mini-computers promise computing power to the end user. Properly viewed, these are not an alternative to, but rather a part of traditional data processing systems. Where and how the information should be stored are questions as important as where the data should be processed. The questions are not only technical but administrative and sociological. (U)

On-line storage costs have dropped steadily, a factor of 10 in 7 years, and the trend will continue. In conventional magnetic storage, the improvements have come from increased storage density. Price-performance has also responded directly to increased competition and higher sales volumes. Hard disk technology has proved to be the mainstream of on-line storage, with occasional forays into new tape technologies, e.g., rotating-head wide videotape, magnetic spools, etc. Floppy disks and tapes most often play the role of tertiary, demountable, personally storable media. (U)

Optical disk technology has so far remained an unfulfilled promise. The technique uses a modulated laser to "burn" on a glass master disk a series of pits following a spiral track like a conventional phonograph record. From this original, a stamping or injection molding master is prepared, and plastic copies reproduced so that the signal-containing pits differentially reflect the "reading" laser beam. Movement of the reading laser can be controlled so that if a machine-readable frame number is included in the video signal and one frame is written per revolution, we have random access and the ability to "freeze" a single frame. Based on a single frame per revolution, the early commercial video disk contained 30 minutes of continuous-play video, or about 55,000 separately readable video frames. (U)

Consumer video disk technology is oriented toward low cost for high volume reproduction, the process is "batched," the whole disk is written and can neither be erased nor updated. Research is underway to adapt the optical read/write technique to a device more suitable to computer applications: immediately readable, erasable and rewriteable, with a capacity of 2x10**11 bits. (U)

If video disks penetrate the mass home entertainment market, then the promise of low cost exists insofar as the computer optical store mimics the home device. Whether home entertainment video disks will be read-only, as at present, or will incorporate a recording capability is difficult to predict. There are market forces in each direction: competition with video tape argues for development of a recording capability; however, the read-only disk is most attractive to the purveyors of program material who have been the driving force to date behind the video disk development (e.g., MCA-Universal Studios). (U)

Computer software, in contrast to the steadily improving price/performance picture for hardware, is increasingly expensive.

In the absence of productivity increases, a predicted scarcity of programmers will accelerate the rising cost of a programmer-hour beyond simple inflation. The dismal picture is worsened yet further by the inevitable movement of software production from the ADP functional specialist to the (generally higher priced) substantive users. This do-it-yourself tendency, fostered by programmer scarcity and abetted by alluringly low-priced, stand-alone hardware, underscores the imperative for improvements in programmer productivity. (U)

Any improvements in programmer productivity will surely come at the expense of "inefficient" use of hardware, e.g., very-high-order interpretive languages, and the inclusion of "off-the-shelf" blocks of code written originally for other purposes and burdened with features inappropriate to the present application. The required large amounts of on-line source will be "wasteful" of storage. (U)

High Order Language (HOL), such as FORTRAN, COBOL, PL/I, JOVIAL, Basic, APL, PASCAL, etc., can improve user productivity by no more than a factor of two. Therefore, we will turn increasingly to Very High Order Languages (VHOL) which may be thought of as a special purpose HOL. When a task is sufficiently specific, and frequent, a special purpose HOL often emerges. The trend to replace programmers and the like with technology and facilitate hands-on interaction by principals may be fostered by development of Agency-unique VHOLs. At the same time we must be alert to the dangers of pursuing a lonely course. The more we specialize the argot of our interactions with information, the less well we can take advantage of progress in the information handling world outside. Database management systems are an important example of a very high order language to which we have already gravitated. The future developments in database management will be the inclusion of data about the data, including access controls. This development will be of vital benefit to the Agency, supporting our need for compartmentation. (U)

Among the issues raised for the Agency by the burgeoning technology are the three S's, Security of data; Scarcity of skilled personnel; and, Sociology of organizational change. Each of these is a challenge to which we all respond, as individuals and as an Agency. (U)

Security and control of information will be deeply affected by the new technologies. Analogies have been drawn between keeping information in the computer and keeping it in a conventional safe. The analogies break down, however, because of: the scale of information stored; the large number of people who know the "combination"; the interconnectivity of some computer systems; the fact that access can be gained remotely, thus removing some physical threat to the penetrator; and, perhaps most importantly, the computer can be turned against itself . . . its own facilities can be used to search through the extraneous and extract the meaningful. In addition, many of the products of the computer are machine-readable and not easily inspectable by humans—magnetic tapes and disks, for example. The danger here is obvious, redoubled by the fact that as storage densities "improve," the mischief which can be caused by a stray piece of magnetic media goes up proportionately. Only now is the Agency facing up to the implications of this increasing threat. On the research front, so-called multi-level secure operating systems have been the perennial focus of attention for a decade or more. Their promise of enforceable compartmentation remains elusive, however. A slightly different attack on the same problem will be encryption of stored data. This will provide a measure of security, compartmentation insofar as facets of a database are "keyed" differently, and quicker destruction and reconstitution as only the keys must be destroyed or re-established. On the brighter side, the indefatigable computer can keep audit trails of who has accessed what information when with an exactitude formerly impossible. (U)

Scarcity of skilled personnel is underscored by a demand which rises each year by over 20%. The severe shortage and increasing demand combine to render non-competitive the wages of government. The increasing mobility amongst personnel, to which this leads, is especially troublesome to the Agency because of its security clearance overhead. A recent survey showed that for computer and telecommunications professionals: 12% are actively engaged in finding a new job, 17% are inactively seeking a new job, and 51% would consider a new position. Only 20% of the respondents indicated they would not consider a new position. The challenge to management is clear: training to provide the reservoir of expertise, and continually improving morale so as to retain our experts. The bright note is that the organizations challenge is the individual's opportunity. (U)

Sociology suggests that as technologies change, particularly information handling technologies, a former apportionment of tasks may no longer be appropriate. New and improved forms of communications, and radically different task durations often suggest a new breakdown or, more likely, a consolidation of task segments. Moreover, information handling technologies are capital intensive with a small cadre of skilled individuals displacing a much larger number of less skilled workers. Thus, organizational structure built around formalisms of grade and span of control may no longer be appropriate. (U)

Many of the organizational changes which will suggest themselves as technology changes can be anticipated. When coupled with healthy skepticism and an appreciation of where technology might lead, new organizational options can be explored. Historically, this has been threatening because change is threatening. To retain (or regain) the vitality of the Agency, we must recognize that organizations are arbitrary social constructions to accomplish an overall job under specific conditions. As the conditions change, so must the organization. Understanding the forces underlying the change is the only way to receive the benefits with a minimum of costly disruption. Here, too, the Agency's challenge can be the individual's opportunity. (U)

To take maximal advantage of the opportunities presented by the technology, there is one thing we all can do. We can become increasingly aware of the information we handle, as distinct from the paper we handle. Consider, for example, administrative memoranda and forms. To communicate administrative information, request information, seek concurrence, or accomplish coordination, we compose a memorandum. As any communication is required over and over, human creativity overlays the few bits of data with poetic variation. The addressee must strip away the semantic disguise to recover the message. Sometimes the process is noisy and the recovery flawed. Additional noise is introduced as the data included by the initiator may not be exactly congruent with the needs of the recipient. Ultimately, a form may be created which structures the communique. Thus, many of our administrative memoranda are basically simple database transactions, which, if the truth be recognized, could proceed directly from keyboard to data base much more efficiently. That is, much of today's word processing is really data processing gone agley. If ever there was the opportunity to "do more with less," it is here. (U)

dda in the 1990's

SECURITY OFFICE OF THE FUTURE (U)

[redacted] OS (C)

[redacted]

Communications—gathering information quickly, assessing it accurately, and using it to make correct decisions. Just as investigations are a major foundation block of OS, rapid communications has always been an integral part of the investigative process. It is in this latter area—the flow of information—that we in OS look forward to great changes in the next decade. (U)

[redacted] allowed our managers to begin shaping our office of the future, focused primarily on the time required for the investigation of prospective staff and contractor employees. Since our mail and clerical process represents a significant but presently unavoidable delay, we attempted to determine if office automation and electronic mail hardware and software could result in a significant shortening of the total investigative time. The initial survey indicates the Delta Date (DD) 7000 series terminal is expected to become the communications workhorse of our future field office and Headquarters network. As envisioned for Agency-wide use, the DD will function as a word processor, a communicating Teletype, and a programmable microcomputer. Within OS, we plan to have terminals assisting in the typing of investigations; electronically speeding the case reports to the Clearance Division; and per-

25X1A

forming routine administrative chores such as manipulating the case control cards. (U)

Coincidentally, the FBI is also putting together a pilot program to automate their field offices. Although the Bureau handles more cases with more agents in many more locations, our approach to common problems is remarkedly similar. (U)

Let's dust off our crystal ball and focus it about 10 years down the road. We'll follow the security processing of a staff applicant living in Phoenix, Arizona in 1990. Once her Personal History Statement arrives in Washington, OPPPM will immediately type it onto a computer terminal. They'll then transfer it electronically to interested components, Medical Services, and Security. (U)

[redacted]

[redacted]

The electronic file of the future will have many advantages we don't enjoy today. More information should become available to a greater number of people much faster. But since discovering a person's background, character, and loyalty is very much a people-oriented business, we anticipate that machines will be of limited value in gathering information—and of great assistance in forwarding, collating, and evaluating data. (U)

We've just barely cracked open our electronic doorway to the future, and what we have seen already poses challenges as well as exciting opportunities. The skilled and dedicated investigators, the "doorbell ringers," will never be less important or necessary than they are today. The challenge, therefore, is to use our new electronic helpers to our maximum advantage—over the next decade and beyond. With the communications and computer power of the CIA supporting us, this Office has the very real possibility of revolutionizing the security investigative cycle from receipt of the case through the collection of background information to the final adjudication. (U)

OC IN THE 1990s (U)

[redacted]OC (C)

Will OC be a viable, dynamic organization, providing an important service to the Agency in the 1990s? We believe so. OC, like all the other components of the Agency, will undergo change during the next decade. Some of our attributes will grow in importance; others may diminish; and a few may disappear. The changes we anticipate, however, will be toward one end—improving the telecommunications service to the Agency and the Community. (U)

International tensions and a renewed interest in strengthening America's defense posture will produce an impetus for new and expanded intelligence activities and products. OC perceives not only a significant growth in information handling (IH) requirements to meet these demands, but diversification in the application of IH systems for intelligence production purposes. New and innovative ways of using technology for

The Office 20 Years From Now

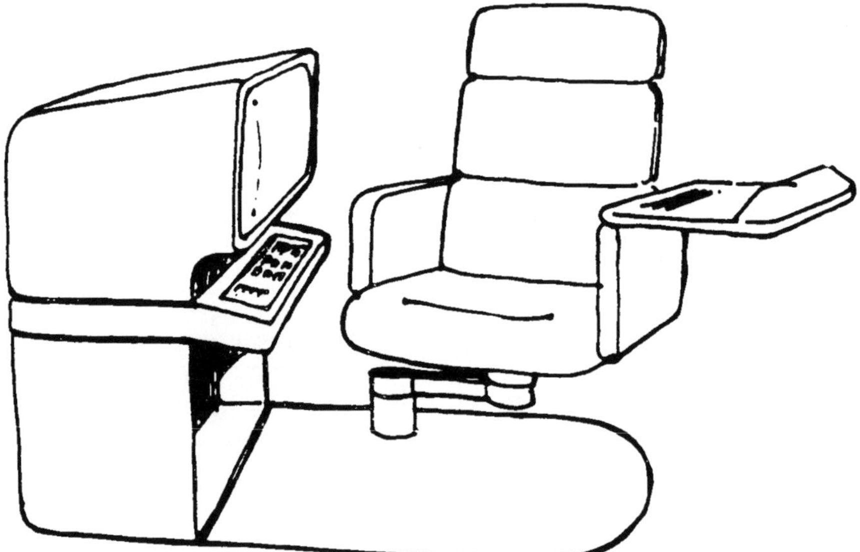

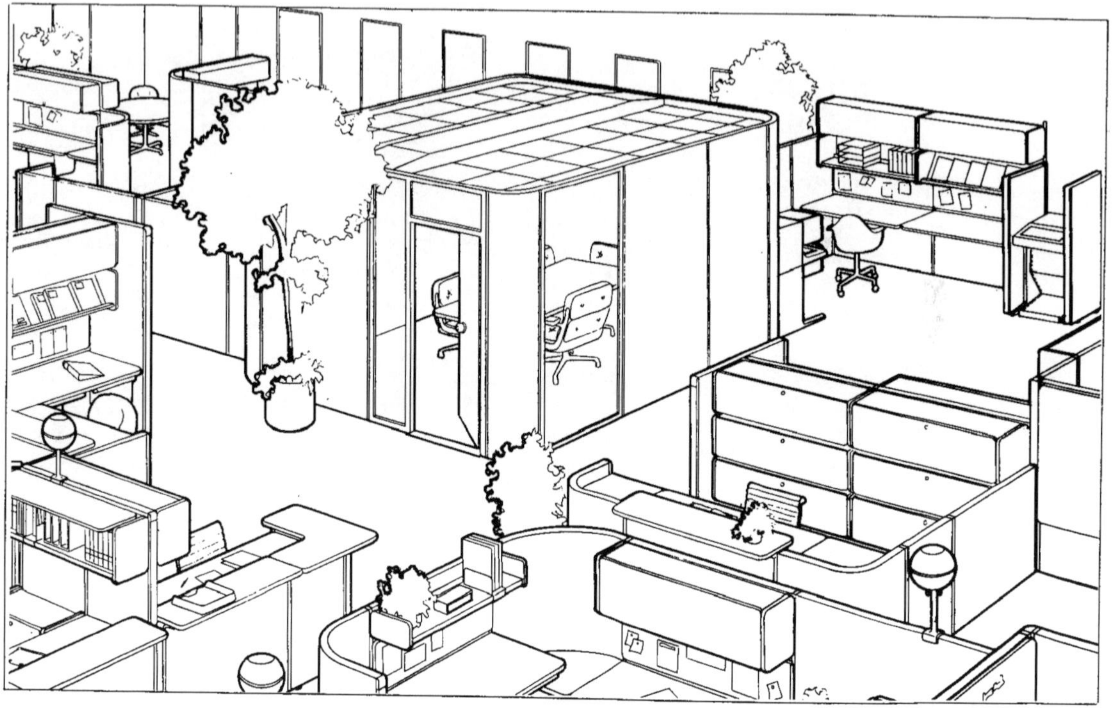

set the effects of scarce resources through increased productivity . . . and . . . maximize the efficient utilization of existing resources through innovation, creative management, and increased utilization of improved technology. . . . (U)

The LIMS project direction is to modernize many obsolete work functions and place OL in a support posture required to service Agency needs in the 1980s and 1990s. (U)

PROJECT MAVIN—OVERSEAS MEDICAL CARE IN THE FUTURE (U)

[redacted] M.D., OMS (U) 25X1A

Medical care overseas, especially in developing countries, is not always up to US standards. Within the United States and in one or two other countries, successful radio networks have been developed to consult and advise patients who live in remote areas. (U)

Project MAVIN (Medical Audio Video Information Network) was conceived as a means of meeting the continuing and crucial need for our overseas employees, dependents, agents, assets, and defectors to have quality medical care readily available. A means of direct audio video communication between patient and physician or physician to physician can help to provide the necessary expertise, access, diagnosis, and care required to fulfill our overseas mission. (U)

At present, MAVIN is in its early conceptual stages. When completed, we envision an overseas person will be able to turn on a television receiver/camera and be able to communicate with a medical consultant at Headquarters. A remote evaluation and examination can then be conducted and further tests or treatment prescribed. (U)

Pilot projects using radio only as well as television have been carried out extensively by the Lister Hill National Center for Biomedical Communications (National Library of Medicine), several medical schools in this country, and abroad. It has proven to be successful, well received by patients, and lifesaving for some. (U)

Due to the nature of our mission, implementation of this program will involve coordination with many Headquarters components. Security and medical privacy problems must be addressed. (U)

Medical research and development in the United States have been occurring at a relatively rapid rate. In medical circles, 5 years is considered "the future"; we envision implementation of MAVIN by 1986. (U)

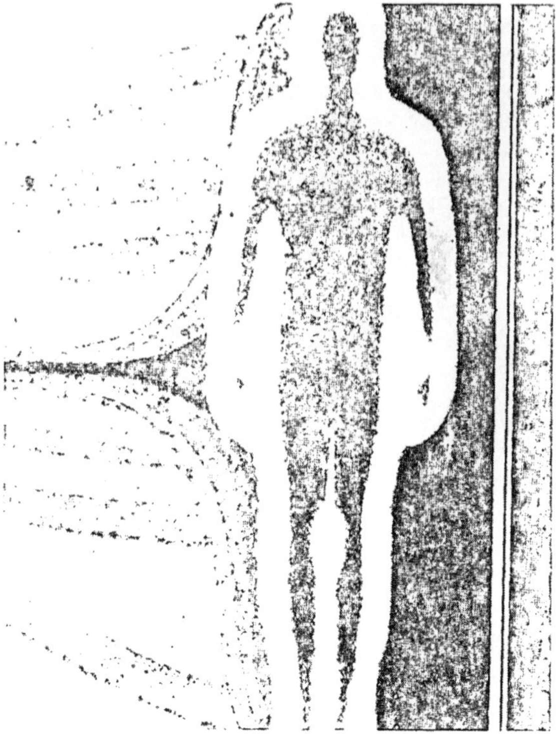

current events

Office of Finance

After several months of soul searching, the Offices of Finance and Data Processing have redirected their efforts from the development of a field financial system for the exclusive support of the [redacted] so-called large DO stations and are now intent upon the development of an automated field financial system which will respond to the needs of all DO field installations. The system is to be developed in part to provide relief to a portion of the DO's field paper-holding issue and to capitalize on the DO's eventual field emplacement of "computer technologies." We hope to report further on this effort in a future *Exchange* article. (U)

Office of Logistics

Construction of the new [redacted] is proceeding generally on schedule. This new building, located [redacted] will house OD&E and OSO/DDS&T. Occupancy is planned for mid-summer 1981 and will go a long way toward alleviating our chronic shortage of space. [redacted]

Office of Training and Education

OTE will conduct its first running of the 16-week Senior Officer Development Course (SODC) on 20 October 1980. This course will provide selected GS-14s and -15s with a comprehensive understanding of the intelligence profession's evolving mission, responsibility, and role in the policymaking process. (U)

The Language School in OTE has received its largest enrollment ever in the part-time language program. The 10 languages (German, French, Spanish, Russian, Italian, Turkish, Chinese, Romanian, Hungarian, and Arabic) have an enrollment of 375 students. (U)

note

I suppose that by now you've noticed that our projections for the DDA's future certainly involve changing technology and its impact. It's difficult to talk technology without a few buzzwords. We tried to keep them to a minimum where we could.

The important thing is that the next 10-15 years are certainly going to involve change for the entire Agency. We can be the agents of that change as easily as we can be the victims of it.

"To the being fully alive the future is not ominous, but a promise; it surrounds the present like a halo."

John Dewey

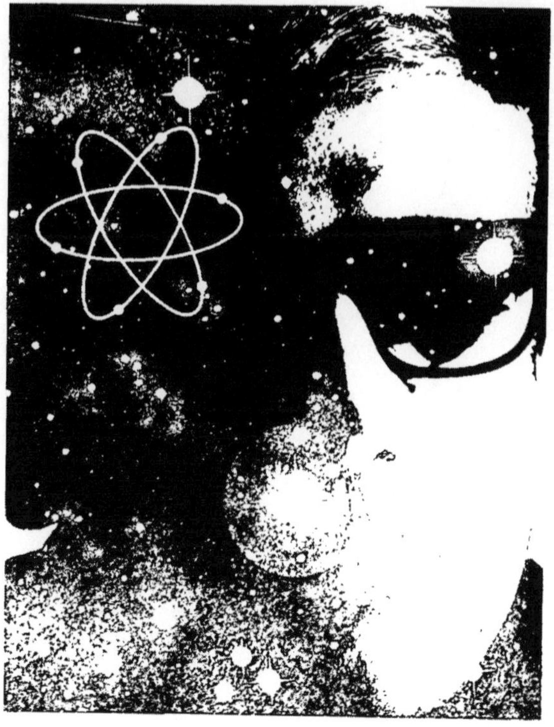

SEE
DDA EXCHANGE READER
SURVEY ON FOLLOWING PAGE.

DDA EXCHANGE READER SURVEY

Each reader of this issue is requested to take a few minutes to answer the following questions. Your responses will help the Editors evaluate the acceptance and usefulness of Exchange. Please fold the completed survey form and staple it so the address on the reverse side shows, then forward it through internal mail. Survey responses should be mailed by 30 November 1980. Results of the survey will be included in a future issue of Exchange.

Please circle the letter corresponding to the most appropriate answer.

1. How much of Exchange do you normally read?

   a) All articles b) Most articles c) An article or two d) Usually don't read it

2. To what degree has Exchange increased your understanding of the Directorate?

   a) Very high b) High c) Moderate d) Low

3. How do you rate Exchange as a source of information?

   a) Excellent b) Good c) Poor d) Very poor

4. What is your opinion of the general quality of Exchange? (writing style, readability, conveyance of message)

   a) Very high b) High c) Low d) Very low

5. What is your opinion of the theme approach versus the standard Exchange format?

   a) prefer theme b) prefer standard format c) prefer a mixture d) no opinion

6. What is your opinion of this particular theme publication, DDA in the 1990s?

   a) strongly like b) like c) dislike d) strongly dislike e) no opinion

7. What topics or subject areas do you suggest for future publication?

   ____

   ____

8. What subject areas do you suggest for future theme publications?

   ____

   ____

   ____

9. Please add any comment or suggestion pertaining to the publication of Exchange.

   ____

   ____

   ____

10. Please check one item in each of the following categories:

    Your grade: GS-14 or above ________

    GS-10 thru 13 ________

    GS-9 or below ________

    Office of Assignment:

____OIS	____OC
____OS	____ODP
____OTE	____OF
____O/DDA	____OL
____Other	____OMS

(PLEASE FORWARD COMPLETED RESPONSES BEFORE 30 NOVEMBER 1980)

Directorate of Administration

secret

February 1981

dda exchange

secret

Nº 49

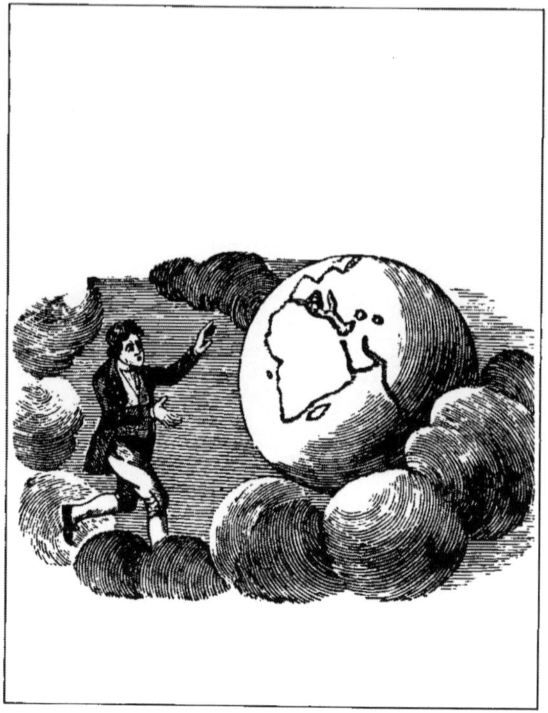

"Only one-third of the people of the world are asleep at any given moment. The other two-thirds are awake and probably stirring up mischief somewhere."

Dean Rusk, 1966

dda exchange

A quarterly publication for the exchange among DDA personnel of ideas, concepts, information, and techniques that are of common interest.

NATIONAL SECURITY INFORMATION

WARNING NOTICE
Intelligence Sources and Methods Involved

Photographs in this issue carry the overall classification of the article in which they appear

staff

index

VOLUME 6, NO. 1

services

NOW WHAT WAS THE QUESTION? (U)

[redacted] OMS (U)

Of every 10 Americans who drink alcohol, one will eventually develop alcoholism. That fact startles most people and convinces many that alcoholism must be increasing by leaps and bounds. Not true. The 10 percent prevalence rate has remained relatively stable over the past few decades. What has changed dramatically is public awareness of the problem's scope. Today alcoholism is recognized as a major health problem, and its victims are treated more openly and more effectively than was the case even 5 years ago. Similarly, although neither alcoholism nor attempts to help alcoholics are new to the Agency, a formal Alcohol Program has been operating within OMS for a little more than two years. (U)

To explain what the Agency Alcohol Program is, it's first necessary to emphasize what it's not: It's not a disguised temperance movement, it's not concerned with social drinking, and it's not dedicated to the proposition that the only good employee is a teetotaling employee. (U)

Now that we've reassured you (we hope) that the Program is not an attempt to dry out the Agency, let's focus more specifically on what the Program is and how it can help you as employee or supervisor, a member of your family, or a coworker. The Program's functions are several. First, it's an educational program which conducts alcohol information programs for all employees and special training sessions for supervisors. It's also a helping program, which offers confidential assistance, treatment referral, and ongoing support to all Agency employees and dependents experiencing alcohol problems. Finally, the Program is a service for management, which provides a constructive way for supervisors to deal with an employee whose job performance is deteriorating. (U)

The Program's success in its helping role depends, to a great extent, on its effectiveness in its role as educator. Before the Alcohol Program can help anyone, it must convince everyone—employees as well as supervisors—of a few basic truths: that alcoholism is a disease, that it can be treated, and that the active concern and cooperation of those around the drinking alcoholic can force even the most reluctant drinker into a treatment program which may well save his * life. (U)

Challenging prejudices and identifying barriers to treatment are major emphases in the Program's educational efforts. Although alcoholism was classified as a disease as long ago as 1956, the suspicion remains that it's a disease nice people don't get. Since most alcoholics are "nice people" like you and me (fewer than 3 percent fit the stereotypical image of a skid-row drinker),

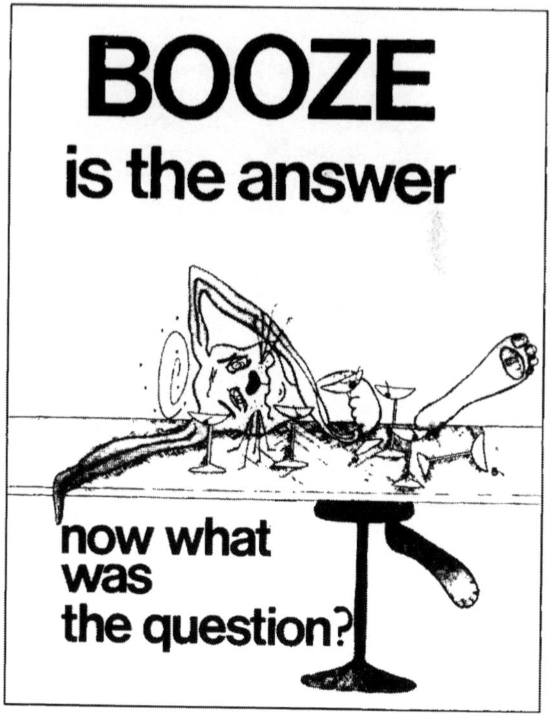

*Alcoholism is an equal opportunity disease. For the sake of convenience and in keeping with the mistakes of history, the masculine pronoun is used throughout. (U)

they go to great lengths to conceal evidence of a disease they believe "nice people" shouldn't have. Well-intentioned friends, family, coworkers, and supervisors unwittingly assist the alcoholic in this life-threatening denial by avoiding and covering up the drinking in the hope that the problem will go away. The problem will not go away. Misguided kindness kills alcoholics, and the Alcohol Program stresses that confrontation by trained people is the only constructive action to take. (U)

For supervisors, job performance is the key to effective use of the Program. If an employee's performance or conduct is less than satisfactory, the supervisor is encouraged to contact the Alcohol Program to determine whether alcohol may be the cause. If alcohol is the problem, a treatment plan is developed for the individual, and the referring supervisor is kept informed of the employee's progress throughout treatment. Timely referrals by supervisors have been critical in saving the jobs of many Alcohol Program clients and the lives of a few. (U)

Supervisory referral is not, however, required for admission to the Alcohol Program. Many employees, concerned about their own drinking or the drinking of a spouse, parent, or teen-aged child contact the Program directly. Many of these self-referrals are seeking an opinion on what they believe to be a developing problem; some are looking for support in handling a problem of long standing; still others want suggestions on treatment facilities. Whatever the request, all are accorded complete confidentiality. (U)

If the Alcohol Program can help you or someone you know by providing confidential assistance or scheduling an alcohol awareness session, call [redacted] (U)

THE 18-WHEELER FLEET OF THE AGENCY (U)

[redacted]
Former Chief, Freight Traffic Branch/
CD/SD/OL

The Agency has many unsung heroes and many who merrily go about their daily tasks within their respective components supporting the mission of the Agency. But none probably affect so many operations as the few Agency tractor-trailer drivers. (U)

Yes, the Agency has nine tractor-trailer drivers assigned to the [redacted] The oddball requirements and overtime obligations of their job would stagger anyone. Last year these nine men each worked an average of 1,000 hours overtime, which is equivalent to six months of work. So in essence, each driver worked one and one-half man-years during 1979. (U)

Agency drivers are required to attend an eight-week tractor-trailer school in addition to a National Safety Council course, a defensive driving course, and lectures on Agency transportation and security procedures. Drivers are required to have a valid state driver's license, pass an annual medical examination, and also pass a Department of Army driving course and examination. (U)

The present corps of drivers ranges in longevity from 1 year to 29 years—all on heavy trucks in the Agency, with the average driver having been on duty with the Agency about 15 years. (U)

Some of the normal daily support which Agency personnel take for granted is provided by the Agency drivers. The tractor-trailer drivers deliver all the administrative supplies and equipment from [redacted] A 42-foot trailer-load, and sometimes two loads, is delivered daily to north dock at Headquarters in the early morning hours. Classified waste, trash, and equipment are hauled to special disposal facilities which are beyond the metropolitan Washington area. The drivers meet an average of four airplanes each week, and deliver

25X1

classified loads throughout the Intelligence Community, that is, to Headquarters, Fort Meade, Pentagon, [redacted] National Security Council, and many other overt and covert sites. (S)

The drivers are briefed on projects that only the operating component personnel are aware of. The drivers, crossing many division and component lines, are cleared for entire programs and not just segments or projects. Their security and dependability must be beyond reproach. (S)

Trips that are over 300 miles require two drivers in order to comply with on-duty requirements of the Interstate Commerce Commission, under which the Agency must operate. No driver can exceed 10 hours straight duty without a minimum rest period, so Agency tractor-trailers have sleeper cabs in order for the drivers to change every 4 hours to preclude stopping with classified or sensitive loads. When classified or sensitive

[redacted] driver, stands beside one of the CD wheelers (U)

equipment is moved, one driver must remain with the truck at all times. Sometimes OS furnishes escorts who follow the truck from loading to unloading. The drivers do not carry weapons. (S)

Agency drivers haul a variety of commodities, such as medicine, flammables, explosives, corrosives, and radioactive materials. Many of these hazardous cargos require special handling, documentation, and routing around populated areas. The Agency must "knock on wood" because our drivers and trucks have never been involved in a major or fatal accident. (U)

The Agency truck fleet last year traveled approximately 300,000 miles to deliver and transport cargo and to meet the aircraft in support of Agency requirements. An Agency driver's life belongs to the Agency because of the oddball hours, many days on the road, and the late hours that must be worked. The next time your office has a transportation requirement for one of the Agency trucks, the drivers would appreciate it if the work could be scheduled from 8 a.m. to 5 p.m., Monday through Friday, in order to free up their weekends and holidays. (U)

THE NEW DELTA DATA SYSTEM (U)

[redacted] ODP (U)

Several years ago, ODP/Applications assembled an Agency-wide group to define requirements for a new series of terminals to upgrade support to users. The result is a new device to provide a variety of capabilities in an interactive environment or a stand-alone mode. Although still in the acceptance stage, the new Delta Data System has attracted wide attention in the Agency and from other government departments. ODP/Processing has about 75 of these systems in a variety of operational situations being tested by programmers and technical personnel. (U)

The Delta 7260T Intelligent Terminal System is a microprocessor-based, user-programmable display terminal system for information applications. The 7260T terminal is provided with or without diskette storage. (U)

The key attributes of the 7260T System are:

- Text Processing
- File Management
- BASIC Language Support (U)

Text Processing functions allow the operator to manipulate and to make alterations and revisions to existing text stored in the terminal's memory. Words, sentences, whole paragraphs, or blocks of text can be moved around or acted on by a variety of text processing functions under operator command or via program control. The manipulated text is highlighted so that it can be easily distinguished from the surrounding text. (U)

File Management functions allow the operator to establish and maintain random or sequential files on diskette. File Management support is a function of the Local Disk Operating System. (U)

BASIC Language support, provided by the BASIC Interpreter, allows users to create programs at the terminal and store them on diskettes or at the host computer. The user programs can be called up from diskette storage or from the host computer via keyed operator commands. Operator interaction with terminal-resident user programs is also performed via a set of keyed commands. (U)

Other key features of the 7260T are:

- Formatted data entry/validation
- Split screen operation
- Full cursor control
- Cursor addressing and sensing
- Paging/scrolling
- Tabulation
- Program function keys
- Operator prompting
- Self-diagnostics
- ASCII/Alternate character sets
- Printer output support (U)

Two of the more unique features will be the addition of diskette storage (not shown in the photograph) and the split screen capability. Diskette storage consists of a separate, dual-drive diskette unit. The 7260 Video Display Terminal supports either of two diskette units, one that accommodates standard 8-inch diskettes and one that accommodates 5-inch mini-diskettes. Both units record data in standard density on both sides of the diskette. Sector length is the same for either size diskette - 560 characters. (U)

The standard diskette provides a formatted data storage capacity of 681,706 characters. The mini-diskette provides a formatted data storage capacity of 191,471 characters. (U)

Disk access is provided by keyed operator commands, by commands received from the host computer, and by commands executed by the resident user program. The host or resident user program can access disks directly without interfering with the display screen. (U)

Split Screen allows the operator to divide display memory into as many as eight discrete segments (splits). Split dimensions are established by the operator via a Split Allocation Table. Splits can be arranged on the screen in any manner, but splits should not overlap. Vertical and horizontal lines displayed on the screen define the boundaries of each split. Each split is functionally independent of the other and may be operating in a different mode. The operator can move between splits via keyed commands. The terminal's memory can be allocated to different splits on a percentage basis. (U)

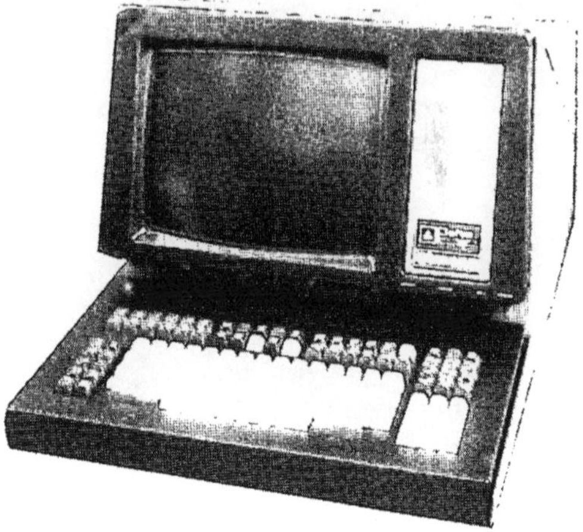

With the above features, the Delta Data promises to be of great value to those who can utilize its full capabilities. It is expected that, over time, a library of user programs will be available for exchange. ODP will act as a clearing house for user developed routines. A word of caution, however; using the 7260 can be addictive. (U)

The basic Delta Data 7260T terminal (U)

information

MOTIVATION IS A BY-PRODUCT OF BELIEF (U)

OMS (U)

Morale, status, and motivation are not really tangible things. We say that the esprit de corps of a military unit is very high; so is that of a terrorist group. The status of a religious leader is very high; so is that of an underworld chieftain in his organization. (U)

Morale and status are by-products of our total environment and how we react to and are seen by ourselves and others in that environment. Motivation is belief in what we are doing. The deeper the belief, the stronger the commitment. Commitment nurtures enthusiasm, energy, and will. This kind of activity promotes achievement and success; hence, status. Achievement and success lead to motivation. (U)

EMPLOYEE MOTIVATION (U)

A job provides full motivational value to the organization when it satisfies all relevant needs which may be present in the person performing it. A balanced job blends all levels of need so that managers may maintain a perspective on group productivity and individual fulfillment. (U)

To accomplish this balance, a voluntary interaction of people at all levels needs to be created. The natural by-products derived from this action are high morale, status, and motivation. (U)

Those who participate in designing these concepts must have an awareness of real needs and conditions, knowledge of the organization and management, and most importantly, freedom of thought. The best results occur when all personnel participate in a free spirit that finds their occupational endeavors and their personal needs, that is, physical, security, social, esteem and self-fulfillment also congruent with their personal, familial, social, occupational, and spiritual philosophy (figure 1). (U)

ORGANIZATIONAL MOTIVATION (U)

An organization and the people within it who believe in their occupational endeavor plan toward a kind of "continual becoming" rather than a final goal. The organization and its people must continually change if the organization is to survive over time. (U)

Past IBM president Tom Watson, Jr. said, "The basic philosophy, spirit, and drive of an organization have far more to do with its relative achievements than do technological or economical resources, organizational structure, innovation, and timing. Three basics paramount to an organization's beliefs should be: respect for the individual, the best customer service possible, and excellence in the pursuit of goals." (U)

Each of us in stating our objectives learns to specify only the "what" and "when"; to avoid the "why" and "how." That is as it should be, provided we have an understand-

Figure 1

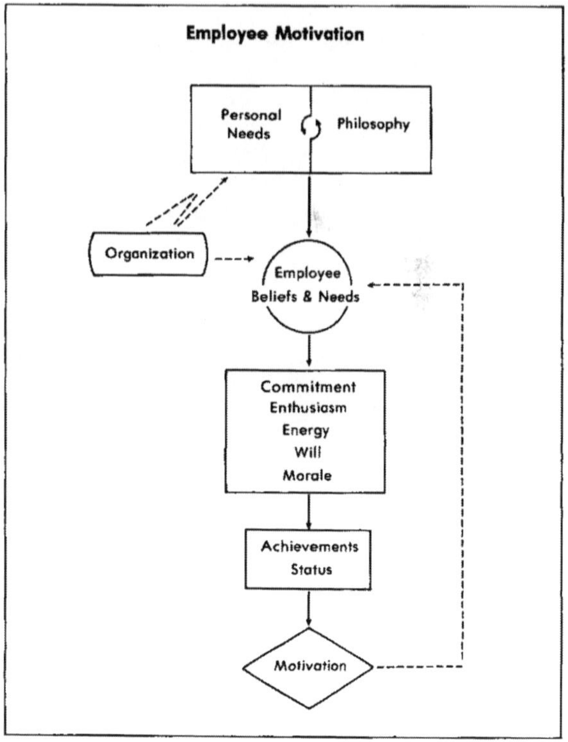

ing of Agency philosophy prior to stating our objectives and goals; that is, what we as an Agency believe, and what the basis is for that belief. Once a mutually agreeable philosophy is reached, we then have a plan against which to weigh our goals and objectives—"why" we have set this goal and "how" will it contribute to the fulfillment of Agency ideals. (U)

For the Agency to succeed, managers must insure that our ethical standards are well defined and that employee work is systematically judged against these standards. Along with this, managers are required to be alert for and anticipate problems and put themselves in a position to cope with the problems when they become real. They do not confine themselves to tactics and strategy alone but must continually evaluate organizational capabilities and intentions. (U)

It is clear that ethical standards must apply evenly and with no exceptions, that these standards take precedence. The fact that everyone knows the rules is a great discipline. It makes managing more effective, and it helps avoid legal difficulties. (U)

While we all should be aware of the major issues involved and the specific choices to be made, an ethical code is the concern of the chief executive—the ideas might come from below, but the responsibility comes from the top. (U)

The ultimate value of any management research an organization undertakes lies in the production of information that enables people to believe in change. The ability to contemplate the future or estimate probability makes people want to change. The idea of change enables people to plan toward a continual becoming—this attitude evokes a maintaining interest to learn (figure 2). (U)

EMPLOYEE AND ORGANIZATION MOTIVATION (U)

Well defined personal and organizational ideals make it less difficult to understand

---

Figure 2 left, Figure 3 right

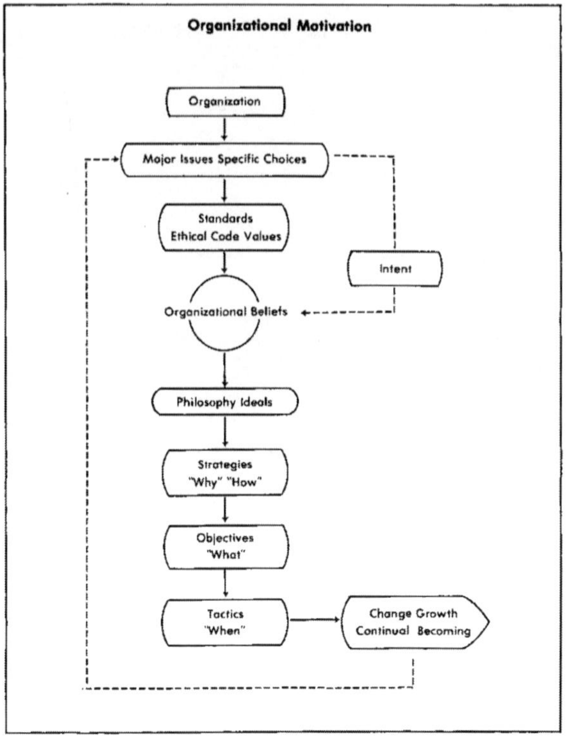
Organizational Motivation
Organization
Major Issues Specific Choices
Standards
Ethical Code Values
Intent
Organizational Beliefs
Philosophy Ideals
Strategies
"Why" "How"
Objectives
"What"
Tactics
"When"
Change Growth
Continual Becoming

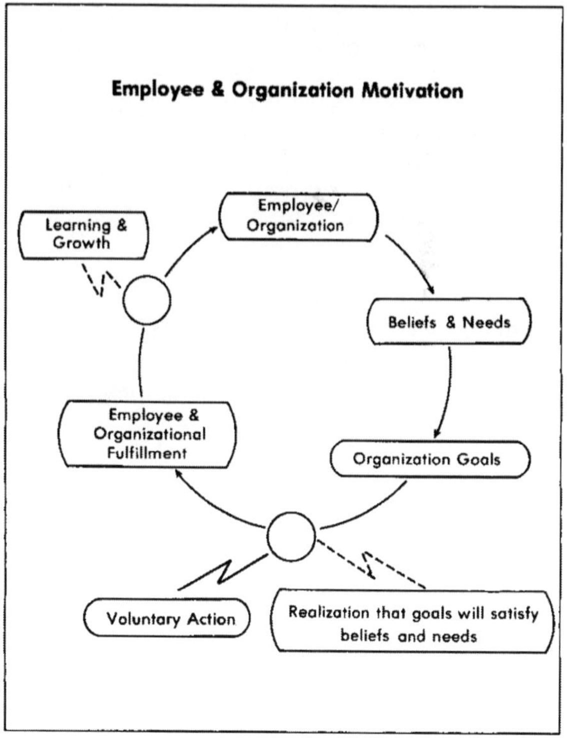
Employee & Organization Motivation
Learning &
Growth
Employee/
Organization
Beliefs & Needs
Employee &
Organizational
Fulfillment
Organization Goals
Voluntary Action
Realization that goals will satisfy
beliefs and needs

and achieve the objectives we personally have chosen and those Agency-directed objectives such as environmental control, community relations, and equal opportunity. This understanding leads to a kind of interest that promotes positive attitudes, evokes enthusiasm, and encourages the motivation that propels people toward voluntary action. (U)

An unending cycle of support is formed, a mutual bond that identifies compatible needs and beliefs which lend themselves to the accomplishment of goals that fulfill both employee and organizational expectations. Hence the organization's and the employee's joint success promote the motivation for the continued growth of both (figure 3). (U)

THE CIA LONG-RANGE PLANNING PROCESS (U)

[redacted]DA/MS (C)

Long-Range Planning in the federal government is coming of age. In an environment of escalating requirements, more complex systems, longer lead times, greater interrelationships among program elements, and heightened competition for budget dollars, both Congress and the Office of Management and Budget are demanding better planning from Agency heads to support budget requests. The CIA Executive Committee's (EXCOM's) response to these pressures was to initiate an Agency-level long-range planning process. The goals of the effort are to provide senior Agency management with a basis for setting directions the Agency will follow in the future and to integrate planning already being conducted at the directorate and lower levels. (U)

With the exception of short-lived efforts in the midsixties and early seventies, there has been no Agency-wide planning process. The budget process includes outyear projections but does not lend itself to true long-range planning because of its focus on resource constraints and solving near-term resource allocation problems. There are planning activities at the directorate and lower management levels that result in multiyear plans for specific activities, such as the Office of Communications Strategic Plan and the Office of Data Processing Long-Range Management Plan, but they have generally lacked Agency-level executive perspective and review and have not been integrated into Agency budget requests. (U)

Beginning in May 1980, an ad hoc Agency Planning Group representing the four directorates, Comptroller, and EXCOM Staff developed a list of five Foreign Policy Issues concerning intelligence topics likely to be of vital interest to U.S. policymakers and five Management Issues concerning how the Agency will conduct its business. In keeping with EXCOM's wish to avoid the planning becoming a purely staff exercise, each of the planning issues was then assigned to a working group comprised of appropriate line managers with the task of developing detailed background material, likely trends, and alternative courses of action. During the months of October and November, the issues were presented to EXCOM by the working groups. (U)

At a final wrap-up session in December, EXCOM reviewed a series of conclusions regarding the planning process. One of the more important questions addressed was what form the planning decisions should take. It had always been anticipated that the results of the planning would be published in the DDCI's guidance letter to the deputy directors for the FY-1983 Program. After a discussion where EXCOM members agreed that the biggest value of planning lay in the exchange of information between the working groups and EXCOM and the resulting discussions that take place among EXCOM members outside the EXCOM forum, it was decided that the guidance should not be in the form of specific decisions on each issue.

Rather, the guidance would reflect those problem areas that should be emphasized in constructing the FY-1983 Program. Actual problem solving will occur at lower managerial levels, in reaction to the issue papers and EXCOM discussions and in response to Program guidance. (U)

EXCOM endorsed a continued planning effort in 1981, building on 1980 planning and again relying heavily on line organizations for input. By formalizing the planning process, Agency managers at all levels are compelled to plan for their future environment, requirements, and capabilities. The informal approach to planning favored by EXCOM provides the membership with a common understanding of the problems confronting the Agency, yet retains the flexibility and responsiveness possible only by retaining our decentralized authorities. (U)

1980 Long-Range Planning Issues (U)

Foreign Policy Issues
- Soviet Union/East Europe
- China
- Third World
- Competition for World Resources
- Our Allies

Management Issues
- Maintaining An Overseas Presence
- Intelligence Collection
- Covert Action
- Communications—Staff and Covert
- Records—Declassification and FOIA (S)

current events

OFFICE OF INFORMATION SERVICES

OIS completed its move to consolidate most of its offices in Rosslyn. The Office of the Director of Information Services, the Records Management Division, and the Regulations Control Division moved in October to the Ames Building, where they joined two of the four branches of the Classification Review Division (CRD). The Office of the Chief, CRD and the remaining two branches will move from the Key Building to Ames Building in the near future. Only the Information and Privacy Division, which completed its move to 1A16 Hqs in August, will remain in the Headquarters Building. (U)

EDITOR'S NOTE:

We want to thank those of you who took the time to respond to our survey in the last issue. The questionnaires are still trickling in, and we promise a comprehensive discussion on the results in our next issue. Generally, though, the responses reflected favorably on the Exchange. (U)

We would also like to thank those of you who offered suggestions for upcoming issues. We are attempting to pursue quite a few of them. If you think you have an interesting article subject, please contact your Senior Editor or Management Staff. We guarantee we'll be interested. (U)

Directorate of Administration

reader feedback

The first year: April 1976 - April 1977

<u>Some Facts and Figures</u>

Number of issues		5
Number of copies requisitioned		
April 1976		325
April 1977		600
<u>VOLUME I</u> (1976 - 3 issues)		
Number of authors		56
Number of articles - O/DDA	17	
OC	7	
ODP	3	
OF	4	
OL	3	
OMS	6	
OP	10	
OS	3	
OTR	6	
DCI	1	
ICS	1	61
Number of Editorial Board Meetings		2

P&PD Estimate of Cost (January 1977 issue)

Camera Time	4
Layout	20
Plate	3
Press	8
Bindery	12
Manhours	47 + material = $1,410

Copies 550

Average cost $2.61 each

OFFICE OF DATA PROCESSING

GS-14 or above

PLEASE ADD ANY COMMENT OR SUGGESTION PERTAINING TO THE PUBLICATION OF EXCHANGE.

---

1. Used now as a self-laudatory, self-congratulatory vehicle for current administration. It is terrible!

2. Very little substance--a glossy showpiece--eliminate it.

3. DDA comments should say ~~somethng~~ SOMETHING--take a stand--not just PR. "In Conclusion"--someone has time on their hands. Why the article on "CB"--waste of time.

4. Some articles are of questionable value--i.e., use of WATS. Pictures need captions--it is very difficult to relate picture to article in many cases.

OFFICE OF FINANCE

GS-9 or below

PLEASE ADD ANY COMMENT OR SUGGESTION PERTAINING TO THE PUBLICATION OF EXCHANGE.

---

1. Very down to earth.

---

2. If published more frequently information would be more timely. Continue use of pictures. Helps to have a face to put a name to.

---

3. How about an article on "Did you know . . ."

OFFICE OF PERSONNEL

GS-14 or above

PLEASE ADD ANY COMMENT OR SUGGESTION PERTAINING TO THE PUBLICATION OF EXCHANGE.

1. Keep up the good work!

2. Keep up the good work; it's a worthwhile publication.

√ 3. Total waste of money--discontinue publication.

---

4. Put in pictures of the authors of the articles.

OFFICE OF SECURITY

GS-14 or above

PLEASE ADD ANY COMMENT OR SUGGESTION PERTAINING TO THE PUBLICATION OF EXCHANGE.

1. Eliminate as soon as possible.

2. To my knowledge nearly no one reads this publication.

3. Some art work--as opposed to photographs only--could enhance the visible impact. Photos and print seem quite staid for the lively nature of this publication.

✓4. I find the publication of minor value and have very limited time to read it. Possibly it is of greater value to those who have the time to read it fully.

5. Would like to see articles re changes in various offices (OC use of ~~Sattelites~~ SATELLITES)

6. I missed some of the earlier publications - perhaps not enough copies were distributed to the various components.

OFFICE OF TRAINING

GS-09 or below

PLEASE ADD ANY COMMENT OR SUGGESTION PERTAINING TO THE PUBLICATION OF EXCHANGE.

1. Most people in the office who do read it comment that it's a waste of time and money.

dda exchange

edited and compiled by
Mitch Anzuoni

Published 2026
Inpatient Press

Distributed to the trade by
The MIT Press